Assessment for Learning in the Early Years Foundation Stage

Jonathan Glazzard, Denise Chadwick,
Anne Webster and Julie Percival

Los Angeles | London | New Delhi
Singapore | Washington DC

First published 2010
Apart from any fair dealing for the purposes of research or
private study, or criticism or review, as permitted under the
Copyright, Designs and Patents Act, 1988, this publication
may be reproduced, stored or transmitted in any form, or by
any means, only with the prior permission in writing of the
publishers, or in the case of reprographic reproduction, in
accordance with the terms of licences issued by the
Copyright Licensing Agency. Enquiries concerning reproduction outside those terms should be sent to the publishers.

SAGE Publications Ltd
1 Oliver's Yard
55 City Road
London EC1Y 1SP

SAGE Publications Inc.
2455 Teller Road
Thousand Oaks, California 91320

SAGE Publications India Pvt Ltd
B 1/I 1 Mohan Cooperative Industrial Area
Mathura Road
New Delhi 110 044

SAGE Publications Asia-Pacific Pte Ltd
33 Pekin Street #02-01
Far East Square
Singapore 048763

Library of Congress Control Number: 2009932258

British Library Cataloguing in Publication data

A catalogue record for this book is available from
the British Library

ISBN 978-1-84920-121-6
ISBN 978-1-84920-122-3 (pbk)

Typeset by C&M Digitals (P) Ltd, Chennai, India
Printed in Great Britain by Biddles Ltd, King's Lynn
Printed on paper from sustainable resources

Contents

Key to icons

Chapter Objectives

Reflective Activity

Case Study

Useful Websites

Key Points

Further Reading

Abbreviations

APP	Assessing Pupils' Progress
CAF	Common Assessment Framework
CLL	Communication, Language and Literacy
DCSF	Department for Children, Schools and Families
DfES	Department for Education and Science
EAL	English as an Additional Language
ECM	Every Child Matters
EEL	Effective Early Learning
EPPE	Effective Provision of Pre-school Education
EYFS	Early Years Foundation Stage
EYFSP	Early Years Foundation Stage Profile
EYPS	Early Years Professional Status
ICT	Information and Communications Technology
LCT	Language Communication and Thinking
NAA	National Assessment Agency
Ofsted	Office for Standards in Education, Children's Services and Skills
PSED	Personal, Social and Emotional Development
PVA	Polyvinyl Acetate
QTS	Qualified Teacher Status
REPEY	Researching Effective Pedagogy in Early Years
SATs	Standard Assessment Tests

SCSE   Self-Confidence and Self-Esteem

SEAD   Social and Emotional Areas of Development

SEAL   Social and Emotional Aspects of Learning

SEN   Special Educational Needs

SENCO   Special Educational Needs Coordinator

TAC   Team Around the Child

Acknowledgements

We would like to express our thanks to all who have contributed to this text. We give particular thanks to the children, students and practitioners of Kirklees, Calderdale and Barnsley who agreed to take part in this work. We hope that this text does justice to their learning stories.

About the authors

Jonathan Glazzard is a Senior Lecturer and Course Leader for Primary Education (Qualified Teacher Status – QTS) at the University of Huddersfield. Prior to this he worked as a primary schoolteacher for 10 years. He champions the importance of formative assessment in his teaching and the need to use assessment to inform planning and teaching. His research interests lie in the area of special and inclusive education.

Denise Chadwick is a Senior Lecturer in early years education and Course Leader for Childhood Studies at the University of Huddersfield. For more than 20 years she taught in primary school environments, working with children in the early years. She believes passionately that the care and education that children receive in their earliest years will without question influence all that they are and achieve in their later years. It is because of this she feels privileged to have taken part in this journey with so many children.

Anne Webster works as a nursery teacher and a local authority consultant. She has extensive experience of working with very young children. She firmly believes that all children have the right to quality pre-school education and has worked tirelessly towards this aim over the past 20 years. She has also supported trainee teachers and she has contributed to training sessions in the university.

Julie Percival is Course Leader for the postgraduate routes to Early Years Professional Status and teaches on the Sector Endorsed Foundation Degree in Early Years at the University of Huddersfield. Julie has been teaching (and learning) for over 20 years and has supported children in a variety of contexts, including special schools, maintained schools, pre-school playgroups and private day nurseries.

Preface

How to use this book

Current education policy stresses the importance of formative and summative assessment in finding out about what children know and can do. This text supports the notion that every child is a unique learner and that children have different starting points in their learning which are often influenced by specific earlier experiences such as home environments and pre-school. Assessment for learning should therefore be positive and celebrate children's achievements. Current educational policy in the early years emphasises the importance of ongoing formative assessment as a way of celebrating individual achievements, children's interests and next possible steps in learning. This text supports this approach and argues that assessment should be informal, regular and should inform future planning.

Theoretical perspectives, key theories and leading pedagogical approaches are addressed in this text. We emphasise within this text a values-led approach to assessment. We stress that children are holistic learners and that practitioners must adopt a principled approach to their practice.

The Early Years Foundation Stage framework (DCSF 2008c) emphasises the importance of practitioners observing children's learning, sharing interpretations and making use of this information to plan for their possible next steps in learning. Assessment should be the starting point for all planning and practitioners should use observation to find out about children's interests, learning needs and achievements (DCSF 2008c). This information can then be used to identify a range of future learning needs. This text addresses the range of ways through which children's achievements can be documented, including the use of self and peer assessment.

It is crucial that practitioners find respectful and innovative ways of involving parents, carers and extended family members in assessment. Parents and carers in particular should be encouraged and supported to contribute to their child's assessment profile and they should have access to these assessment records. The voice of the child within assessment is also paramount and practitioners should privilege the views of children in the assessment process. This text addresses these important issues and provides practical suggestions for involving parents, carers and children in assessment.

The use of summative assessment in the Early Years Foundation Stage is discussed and this text provides practitioners with useful guidance on ways in which summative assessment data can be analysed. The Early Years Foundation Stage Profile is discussed in terms of what it is and how it can work. The role of assessment for identifying and supporting children with Special Educational Needs is also considered.

The current move to increase the emphasis placed on teacher assessment within Key Stage 1 is welcomed. Practitioners working within Key Stage 1 should document children's achievements in a range of ways rather than relying on the outcomes of formal tests. There is real potential to learn from best practice in the Early Years Foundation Stage so that Key Stage 1 practitioners are able to build on the approaches to assessment used within the early years. This text offers some practical suggestions for ways in which each child's assessment journey can be continued.

Within this text we make use of several key features. These are listed below:

Case Studies: The case studies presented in this book draw on examples of practice from a range of settings, including playgroups, nurseries and schools.

Reflective Activities: Reflective activities enable students to think critically and rigorously about their practice. They invite readers to draw on their understanding of the purpose and process of assessment and challenge their practical application of this learning to a range of activities. The activities are creatively designed to engage readers in a range of assessment strategies and encourage skills in making personal reflection on their learning, for further professional practice.

Key Points: The key points are included as a way of challenging understanding about the concept of assessment and the wider discussion of this topic that exists within each chapter. They have been thoughtfully written to encourage consideration of certain aspects of teaching and learning that impact upon making effective assessment, such as organisation of the learning environment and systems for gathering assessment. The points identify useful reminders about making observation of children in learning contexts, promoting discussion with other professionals about evidence that is gathered and making forward planning to enhance children's opportunities for further learning.

Further Reading: The authors have included signposts to additional texts and literature that offer additional understanding and opinion about early years practice and related theory, linked to making assessment with children.

Useful Websites: The websites that have been listed at the end of each chapter are often linked to the specific chapter content and present an opportunity for making extended personal research.

This book is directed at students on a range of (QTS) Qualified Teacher Status, Early Years Professional Status (EYPS) and early years courses. The aim of the text is to deepen students' understanding of assessment for learning and to stimulate their thinking about how they might approach assessment within their own practice.

1

Assessment for learning: theoretical perspectives and leading pedagogy

Jonathan Glazzard and Julie Percival

Chapter Objectives

This chapter focuses on:

- The ideas of key theorists and the implications of this body of knowledge for your own practice.
- Leading pedagogical approaches and the use of these approaches in your own practice.

Why is it important to include a chapter on theorists, theories and leading pedagogy? As a practitioner, you might question the relevance of theory to your own practice. All you really want are 'tips' that will help you to do your job better. However, there is a significant difference between being a practitioner and being a reflective practitioner. It is vital that you have knowledge of the underpinning theories upon which your practice is based. This helps to articulate your practice more effectively, and, more importantly, knowledge of the underpinning theories helps you to know *why* you are doing *what* you are doing. Clearly, within one chapter it is not possible to cover all the theories and this chapter does not seek to do this. Instead, this chapter focuses on a small selection of ideas that have the potential to have a major impact on your practice.

Leading approaches and theories

This section does not attempt to focus on all the approaches and theorists who have relevance to early years education. Instead this section provides a brief synopsis of well-known approaches to early years practice and key learning theories which underpin effective practice. The relevance of these approaches and theories to assessment will be highlighted.

The Montessori approach

Montessori was born in 1870. Montessori emphasised the importance of children learning through their senses through practical tasks, which children worked through individually. She introduced a range of self-correcting teaching apparatus, which enabled children to correct their mistakes. You may have seen plastic trays for sorting shapes into specific compartments. This is an example of the Montessori approach. The role of the adult within this approach is to observe children and guide them through their misconceptions. Careful assessment is therefore central to the Montessori approach.

The Steiner approach

Rudolph Steiner set up his first school in Stuttgart in 1919 for the children of the cigarette factory workers. Steiner emphasised the importance of nature in early education. He believed that children should be encouraged to play in the mud and sand and that they should explore the properties of water. He emphasised the importance of children learning through their senses and the importance of rhythm, song and rhyme. Steiner believed that the formal process of learning to read should begin after the age of 7. He stressed the importance of learning through play, especially imaginative play, and the importance of cookery in the curriculum. Steiner emphasised the importance of play that is unstructured by adults.

The role of the adult within this model is to act as a guide and mentor to young children. Therefore adults may play alongside children and children will learn through imitation. Thus, in an art activity a practitioner might work alongside children creating their own painting. In this example, the adult models key skills discretely and the children absorb these, thus moving their learning forward. The adult acts as a mentor within the Steiner model and this has implications for assessment.

It is not difficult to see elements of this approach interwoven in the statutory Early Years Foundation Stage (EYFS) framework. Therefore, as a student it is important that you plan frequent opportunities for children to learn in the outdoors and that you value the learning which takes place through play. The role of the adult within children's play is also important within this model. Steiner believed that adults should not direct or control children's play. He believed that children should set their own agendas for their play. However, within this model, practitioners should support the play and children will then learn through imitation. You may be familiar with the term *child-initiated, adult-supported learning* and this is an application of Steiner's model.

 Reflective Activity

Imagine that a group of children are engaged with fantasy play based around the Gingerbread Man. You observe their play closely and you notice that some children are not using expressive language and not taking turns in their communication. You ask the children if you can play with them and you decide to be one of the characters in the story. You start to model the use of expressive language. You speak in a similar way to the characters in the story and you model turn taking in communication.

- How important is the assessment process in this scenario?
- How did the practitioner support the children's learning?

Reggio Emilia

Loris Malaguzzi (Malaguzzi 1996) was the founder of the Reggio Emilia approach. He believed that there are a hundred ways in which children learn and express themselves. Assessment should therefore seek to capture all the 'languages' of expression, and learning can be evidenced through a range of forms including play, language, art, drama and the written word. Within this approach it is the role of the practitioner to co-construct learning alongside the child. Assessment is used to identify where support is needed. There is no written curriculum. Instead, the child is seen as the starting point for the curriculum. Practitioners can therefore use assessment to identify children's interests.

Te Whariki

Te Whariki is the national curriculum for early childhood in New Zealand and it was developed by Margaret Carr and Helen May. Literally translated, 'Te Whariki' means a woven mat on which every-one can stand. The mat represents central principles, strands and goals into which each setting is able to weave its own curriculum to meet local needs. The curriculum is mandatory in all government-funded settings. The broad *principles* focus on empowering the child and a focus on the holistic learner. Positive relationships and strong partnerships with families and communities form part of the core principles. The five *strands* include developing a sense of well-being, developing a sense of belonging, and making contributions to learn-ing, communication and exploration. Thus, play-based learning and active learning are central to the curriculum. This approach draws on sociocultural theory, which assumes that learning is socially con-structed between children and adults and between children and their peers. The role of the adult is to scaffold the child's learning. Therefore accurate assessment is necessary so that learning tasks can be pitched at the correct level within the child's capabilities. 'Minute by minute' adults are asked to listen, watch and interact with a child or groups of children. In addition, 'intelligent' observational assessment gathered over time, plays a crucial role in enabling practitioners to identify missing links within a child's learning journey. Appropriate intervention, scaffolding and support can then be pro-vided to enable the child to progress. The curriculum is not fixed and through evaluation of provision and careful application of prin-ciples, the programme will be modified to better meet the needs of particular communities of children.

Vygotsky: a social constructivist perspective

Vygotsky proposed that children could reach higher levels of understanding if someone who is more able supports them through their *zone of proximal development*. This is the gap between what chil-dren can do unaided and what they can potentially do if they are supported. Essentially, an adult or peer *co-constructs* the learning with the learner until the learner is able to complete the task independently. Vygotsky believed that children's development (cognitive, social and language development) is enhanced through social interaction. This contrasts with Piaget's views of the child as a solitary learner. Jerome Bruner used the metaphor *scaffolding* as an analogy to explain how adults or more able peers can support children's learning. The *scaffolder* supports the child by supporting, guiding, modelling and questioning until the child is able to complete the task independently. The role of the scaffolder is to co-construct the learning with the child until the child is able to function without the support. Learning in this way takes place in a social context and language exchanges facilitate learning. Vygotsky highlighted the role of language in learning and the importance of language as a tool for constructing thinking. He believed that social interaction is a vital part of the learning process.

What are the implications of this approach for assessment for learning? As a student on placement, it is essential that you plan tasks which are within the child's zone of proximal development. You need to know where children are in their learning (actual developmental level). This knowledge is derived from your assessments of each individual child. You therefore need to track children's progress against the EYFS framework. You need to plan challenging tasks that are pitched slightly above the child's actual level of development in order to move children through their respective zones of proximal development. You can do this by identifying the child's 'next steps', using the EYFS framework. Providing that adult or peer support is available you can then provide support to enable children to reach their proximal levels of development. The learning is essentially co-constructed between the adult and the child. This is a fundamentally different concept to the learning being 'directed' by a more knowledgeable other.

 Reflective Activity

Your observations show that Matthew is able to select the correct numerals to represent 1 to 5. You now want to move him forward in his learning.

(Continued)

- Use the EYFS framework to identify Matthew's actual development.
- Use this same framework to identify the next steps for Matthew.
- Think carefully about how you will support Matthew to reach his proximal level. How will you introduce the new concepts in a way that allows both you and Matthew to co-construct the learning rather than you directing the learning?
- How will you assess Matthew's progress?

 Key Points

- Use observation and other forms of assessment to identify children's actual levels of development. Use the EYFS framework to plan their next steps. Plan activities to address children's next steps. Activities should be pitched at a level higher than the child's actual level of development to ensure sufficient challenge. However, some consolidation or reinforcement tasks will also be necessary.
- Observe children engaged in child-initiated and adult-led learning. Identify any misconceptions and provide appropriate support to enable children to progress through their respective zones of proximal development.

Case Study: Parents as partners: local authority context

Read the following case study of a local authority project. A local authority practitioner has written the case study, As you read the case study think carefully about how social constructivist theory has been draw on to support work with the parents. (As you may know, Petwari is the local dialect of Punjabi.)

The practitioner devised workshops for small groups of parents where they listened to 'sounds from home' boxes. Everyday cardboard boxes were filled with a range of different materials that could be found in the home: for example, pasta, rice, wooden pegs, stones, spoons and coins. The parents were encouraged to shake the boxes, talk about the sounds they could hear and make phonic links with the words describing the materials. No graphemes were introduced, as the point was to encourage parents to 'tune into sounds'.

The parents became very enthusiastic about exploring sounds and linking them to words and a second workshop was held for them to feed back what they had done at home with their children. Examples of the learning points raised by the parents themselves were:

- 'B…b..b.. we've got bath and banana and books and bangles at home!'
- 'In English, it's r r r r rice but in Petwari it's ch ch ch chowel. My son knows both.'
- 'She put the stones and then marbles in a bucket and played with them in the garden.'

Above all there was a message for the parents about the importance of their involvement with their children at home. As one parent summarised:

'Now I know that this learning can be fun. It doesn't have to be boring and serious. Last night I sat on the bed with my son and we listened to the sound of the owl. We made the sound. Is that early phonics?'

Many questions are raised by this seemingly simple activity:

- How does this way of working with parents or carers draw on socio-constructivist theory?
- It is significant that the parents were supported to develop a language for talking about phonics and their children's learning in a way that was accessible and gave them confidence to express themselves. Can you investigate why language and communication is so important in social constructivist theory?
- Why is **doing** together and then **sharing** the experience so important for learning?
- How did the practitioner show that the learning at home was valuable?
- If you judged it to be the right time, how might you build on this enthusiasm and encourage the parents to document the learning at home?
- How might the information about children's learning at home be celebrated within the setting?

Piaget: a constructivist perspective

Piaget believed that children learn when they actively construct their own learning by interacting with physical objects in their environment. He stressed that children construct their own understandings as a result of interacting with resources that stimulate their thinking. For Piaget, 'physical activity leads to mental stimulus, which in turn leads to mental activity' (Morrison 2009: 116). According to Piaget, children take in (or *assimilate*) new learning. However, children must adjust existing thought structures before they can *accommodate* new information. Children may have difficulty accommodating new experiences if these are radically different from their past experiences, and as a result of this Piaget stressed that new experiences should relate to and connect with past experiences (Morrison 2009). This state is known as *disequilibrium*. If new learning is accommodated as reality, then *equilibrium* occurs. Morrison (2009) provides an example of this theory applied to practice. Very young children learn to recognise dogs and build up a mental representation of these (assimilation). When they notice a cat for the first time they may refer to it as a dog because it has four legs and a tail (disequilibrium). They must build up a mental representation of 'cats' which excludes dogs (accommodation) (Morrison 2009).

How might this model be used to help us understand children's misconceptions? How might approaches to assessment inform you about children's misconceptions? Piaget's work has not gone uncriticised, particularly his staged theory of children's development, which has led some scholars to argue that Piaget largely underestimated children's abilities (see the work of Margaret Donaldson, for example, in Donaldson 1978).

Schemas

The work of Piaget and his theories of child development influenced Chris Athey's work on schemas. Athey was interested in the development of different behaviours in early childhood. Schemas represent a set of repeatable patterns of action on objects. Therefore in the early years children learn to develop a 'sucking' schema and they apply this to a range of objects. As they develop, children start to use a wider range of schema. For example, they may develop a throwing or banging schema. Children may then start to apply different schema to specific objects in order to make generalisations about which objects can be sucked, banged, thrown, etc. The role of the practitioner in the early years is to observe children closely to see which schema they are using. The practitioner can then provide experiences that enable children to use their existing schema in order to extend the breadth of their learning. Children's patterns of play change and children will develop interests in different schemas. Children may develop an interest in objects that rotate (rotation schema) or they may enjoy placing objects inside containers (enveloping and containing schema). Some children develop an interest in creating boundaries or working within boundaries (enclosure schema) and others may enjoy moving things about in different ways (transporting schema). Children may develop a range of schemas and practitioners should make use of careful observation to identify the specific schemas which children have developed an interest in. Practitioners should then extend the child's range of experiences within specific schemas.

The example below illustrates how children's schemas can be incorporated into the planning process. In this example the child is developing his understanding of the 'connecting' schema. In this particular schema, children develop a genuine interest in joining materials together:

 Case Study: Nursery: Joshua, aged 3 years and 6 months

Joshua was frequently observed on the cutting and sticking table joining things together. He loved to use glue and he would spend a great deal of time cutting out paper shapes and sticking them onto paper. He loved to use PVA glue and he also enjoyed using the glue sticks. Joshua would frequently come into the setting on a morning with collages he had made. The practitioner was keen to extend Joshua's experiences of joining. She introduced staplers into the writing area and she modelled to Joshua how to use one. She showed him how to use sticky tape to join pieces of paper and she modelled how to use large needles to sew pieces of fabric together. Joshua experimented with the range of joining techniques and enjoyed the new learning that was taking place.

- How important was observational assessment in this example?
- How did the practitioner extend Joshua's learning within the specific schema?
- How did the practitioner take a lead from the child?
- How might this schema be further developed in the outdoor provision – for example, using ropes and crates? Can you think of other ways of extending Joshua's learning within the connecting schema?

Some further scenarios relating to schema are described below.

Case Study: At Home: Amy, aged 1 year and 2 months

Amy sat in her highchair watching what was going on in the room. She used her right hand to reach out and grasp a spoon. She banged it on the table and then released it. Her mum came over and said her name, 'Amy'. Amy reached out to her with both hands, her mum lent over, and she grasped her hair. Her mum released her hair. Amy then started reaching out and grasping the rattle toy, which was fixed to her highchair; she gurgled with delight as she did this. Over the next hour Amy repeatedly grasped at the rattle and picked up the spoon.

Amy is showing signs of a sensori-motor schema around grasping. How could you use heuristic play to provide Amy with a wider range of experiences? How important is assessment in this scenario?

 Case Study: Children's centre: Jamie, aged 3 years and 4 months

Jamie sat on the floor with an assortment of objects and a variety of different containers. He picked up a small wooden car, and looked at it and put it down again. He picked up a large box and looked inside. He put the box down and looked around him at all the other objects. He picked up the box again and looked into it. He then picked up the wooden doll and put it inside the box. He looked into the box. He then started to collect a selection of the other objects and put them inside the box, looking in at them after each one (for example, a brick, a shell, a pebble, a wooden doll and a piece of string). He stood up and went over to the window with his 'treasures' where some children were looking out of the window. He stood behind them taking out objects from his box, looking at them and putting them back. After repeating this several times he took them over to his key worker, sat next to her on the floor, and got each treasure out and laid it on the floor, smiling at her after each object. When they were all out, the key worker said, 'What a lot of lovely things.' Jamie put all the objects back in his box and went over to the construction area, where he put his box down and started selecting bricks to build with. Later on that day, Jamie used a bag to carry around some pencils, crayons and objects from Small World play sets, such as toy cars and farm animals.

Jamie is showing signs of an enveloping schema. How might you extend the range of experiences which Jamie is exposed to develop further his learning within this area? How important is assessment in this scenario?

Key Point

- Observe children closely and extend their experiences within a specific schema.

Metacognition and metaplay

Piaget researched and theorised (or described) children's development of mental processing. He considered children's thinking as mental operations carried out in response to the environment in which the child finds him/herself. Building on this work, other cognitive psychologists have looked at how children process information and store it. Problem solving and memory development have been extensively researched, and this work can contribute to our understanding of learning and suitable methods of assessment.

Of particular interest is metacognition. This body of work aims to help us understand how we become aware of our own mental operations – our ability to process information, store it, retrieve it and use it to build new learning. Very young children can be supported to become aware of how they learn. Children process information and develop their understanding by 'doing' (as kinaesthetic learning), or by careful 'listening' (auditory learning), or by 'seeing' (visual learning) – if not a combination of all three. Provision for multi-sensory learning is a fundamental recommendation of the EYFS Practice Guidance (DCSF 2008b), and the child's growing awareness and control of these channels supports the assessment for learning process.

If children can be aware of themselves as conscious learners, then their conscious self-assessment becomes possible. This ongoing, formative assessment recognises children as competent learners from birth and requires adults to observe carefully, not only for the skills and knowledge children acquire but also *how* they are acquired. When we assess how children learn it follows that their understanding of their own learning processes (strengths and limitations) and active selection of particular approaches should be part of our assessments (and in turn our planning for provision). Assessment for learning is not a 'bolt on' but an opportunity for 'the learner to judge for him or herself how things are going' (Carr 2001: 93). This active involvement challenges the deficit model approach (what doesn't this child know?) and becomes 'a narrative about confidence and optimism' (Carr 2001: 103).

This layer of thinking about thinking can be seen when children are immersed in their play. As the theme for the role-play unfolds, children may step back and structure what has happened and what will happen next, who will be who, where the play will be situated, and how issues could be resolved. This metaplay (see, for example, Trawick-Smith 1998) shows how children actively direct their learning through ongoing assessment of what has gone before (learned already) and how the play could be extended in the future.

Discourse theory

More recent theories associated with terms like 'poststructuralism' and 'critical theory' may perhaps seem irrelevant to the practical realities of everyday practice in an early years setting. Why would you want to consider these theories when studying the assessment of young children? Surely it is the individual children that we as practitioners need to understand rather than the wider structures in society implied by these theorectical positions.

Early years practitioners work in diverse settings with children who live in and contribute to a multiplicity of diverse communities. Every practitioner in the setting has the power to shape the child's development to a greater or lesser extent. How we understand this diversity can have a significant impact on our ability to assess children's abilities and needs fairly. We also find ourselves considering what 'best practice' in assessment should look like. We may even have in mind what a 'good' child looks like and should do. Sometimes the criteria for such judgements seem clear and sometimes our assessments are made on the basis of assumptions, apparent common sense and received wisdom.

When we talk about children and their development, a framework of feelings, values and understandings of what we believe to be true helps us to decide:

- What to say and do.

- What to see as normal.

- What to see as different.

This complex framework or guide, built on our use of language, ideas and ways of doing things, is termed *discourse*. For some theorists we are *subject* to and at the same time contribute to the dominant, most popular discourses. These in turn determine what and how we think, feel and understand. For others, each of us can *select* from a range of discourses and contribute to their formation and currency. Either way, discourses together produce 'regimes of truth' (Foucault 1980) that guide our practice.

Why would this be relevant to the assessment of babies and young children? You will have heard people discussing someone – a particular person associated with a group who is 'other' than us. Perhaps the topic has been whether someone is doing the right thing or how a particular group of people always seems to behave in a certain ways. Probably the conversation will draw on a collection of ideas (discourses) as the person being discussed is essentially judged and allocated an identity in the social world.

These ideas about identity are passed on through the media, and through conversations, just like the ones you might overhear or, indeed, take part in! It seems like incidental chatter. However, other conversations are much more important to us and influence how we are able to form our identity and live our lives. Doctors, midwives, Sure Start workers, researchers, early years practitioners, teachers and lecturers all use discourses to organise their thinking and their work. Discourses, it is argued, influence how we look at children, what we understand to be their needs and their strengths, how we prioritise what is important for them to learn, and what it is that we should take the time to assess.

Why are discourses any more interesting than stereotypes and metaphors? Surely we all need these shorthand ways of making connections between the known and unknown? 'Knowing' things means having some power either over yourself or over other people. Professional knowledge can sometimes mean that you will make life or death decisions for other human beings. If those decisions are determined by truths that have evolved to ensure power and status stay with in a certain group in society, then there is a lack of fairness and equity for others.

Being aware of these theoretical propositions should support you to reconsider your thinking about children and your assessment routines, both formal and informal. It is not just an interesting exercise, completed in the abstract as part of an academic assignment. Sometimes in early years, discourses can guide our behaviour in such a way that injustice or discriminatory practice occurs. Children may be excluded or misjudged and, as a result, may have limiting learning opportunities or be subject to disrespectful care routines.

MacNaughton and Williams (2009) write very practically and in detail of specific teaching techniques that enable practitioners to challenge the stereotypes that build up around certain discourses. Your assessment priorities should reflect your thinking about children's learning. This thinking should be informed not only by social constructivist theories (Vygotsky, for example) but also by the transformational theories from which discourse theory is drawn. The message is that through a deeper understanding of children's lives (voiced by children, families and practitioners), you can make informed choices in your work and avoid injustice wherever possible. In this way each child may be nurtured to reach their potential.

 Reflective Activity

Gather together a range of advertising aimed at adults but marketing products for children. You may find material that relates to formula milk, baby foods, nappies and toiletries. What have you been able to find relating to toys for babies, toddlers and young children?

Consider your chosen images carefully.
What language is used?
What images are used?
What do these images suggest?

Perhaps it seems as if babies are cute and that if adults apply the right product in the right situation, all will be well. One 'truth' could be that you can assess or diagnose, apply the treatment or buy the solution off the shelf and the desired outcome will automatically result. This is a modernist, scientific way of thinking that implies you can always link cause and effect. Another 'truth' we may glean from advertising is a sense of what normal families look like and do.

Can you list what the adverts tell us about 'normal' families? Do you ever compare yourself to the images you see? How do you feel? What are the links to assessment? You want to assess and take the right professional action to meet the child's needs. But what are the assumptions that underpin assessment methods?

- What does a 'normal' child look like?
- Who decides what is developmentally appropriate and why?
- What is it important to assess (and then plan for)?
- Who does the assessing and why?
- How does our understanding of 'difference' impact on assessment?

Any theory is only a tool for thinking and systematically explaining aspects of our world. A theory is only a possibility, yet it can be argued that some hold greater sway than others. How might the power of some theories have an impact on your assessment practice?

Key Point

- Use theory to ask questions about your assessment practice so that you and your team arrive at ways of understanding and working together that give space for the technical and the statistical, but also the richness of relationships and learning. Above all, assessment practice should be just and inclusive and not close down other ways of looking at and listening to young children.

Leading pedagogy

This section provides an overview of some key pedagogical approaches that underpin effective early years practice. Links to the importance of assessment are made within the sections.

Heuristic play

Elinor Goldschmied and colleagues (Goldschmied and Jackson 2004) developed this particular approach to supporting the learning of very young children. The word 'heuristic' is derived from a Greek word 'eurisko', meaning 'I discover' or 'I find', and heuristic play sessions are specifically organised times of the day where groups of children (usually between the ages of 10 and 20 months) are offered particular conditions for discovery learning and concentration. The area for play will be sectioned off and resourced with a range of natural and manmade materials that can be arranged on the floor area or offered in sturdy 'treasure' baskets. Space to shuffle, crawl or 'toddle' and select objects is important. Sufficient quantities of objects should be available to ensure disputes arising from sharing are kept to a minimum.

Adults have a very particular role in this play. Their closeness and alertness is important so that children feel settled and safe to explore. Unobtrusive rearranging of objects to support the uninterrupted flow of thinking is also helpful. Unlike most other times of the day, adult talk is not a feature of these sessions. Observation is vital. The practitioner needs to build a picture of the type of thinking the child is using and the concepts being explored. This assessment then enables the practitioner to refine the selection of objects made available to the children.

For the child, there is no right or wrong way to handle the objects: there is only the opportunity to decide how to explore, with what actions and other objects. The sessions can last for 40 minutes, with children deeply engrossed in almost silent exploration. Children develop their own 'learning tools' (Stroh and Robinson 1998, in Hughes 2006: 60), and it is their own appreciation of the effectiveness of their actions (using these tools) and their developing understanding of certain concepts that give children a sense that they are in control of their own learning.

Heuristic play is potentially inclusive and anti-discriminatory. The assessments made through patient observation are unique to each child. The practitioner resources and structures the session carefully beforehand, but the children self-assess, regulating their own learning, and practising how to think and explore.

Voice of the child

The contemporary view of children recognises children as citizens with their own rights. The United Nations Convention on the Rights of the Child was signed by the UK in 1990. Article 12 provides children with the right to express their opinion and to have their views acted upon. This has implications for assessment. Effective practitioners should seek children's views about their learning and involve them in self-assessment. As practitioners, we must not underestimate the voice of the child in either the planning process or the assessment process. We must ensure that children's voices are heard, that we regularly consult them and see them as competent individuals who have a right to express their views on all aspects of learning. The *Every Child Matters* agenda emphasises the importance of the voice of the child, and the rights of children to have their say and have their voices both heard and acted upon are now enshrined in legislation. Involving children in the assessment process will empower children to take control of their own learning. A key challenge for practitioners will be to develop the means through which children with profound disabilities can be consulted in the planning and assessment processes.

Planning from children's interests

The children's interests are the best starting point for your planning. Within the Reggio Emilia approach from northern Italy, the child's interests are the starting point for an 'emergent curriculum' (Rinaldi 1995: 102). This approach is gaining popularity across the world, and some settings have adopted the High Scope approach where children plan their daily activities with a practitioner. How important do you think assessment is within this process? It is important that you tune into children's interests. Some of these interests will emerge through their play and it is therefore important that you observe children in a range of contexts in order to find out about their interests. You need to spend time talking to children about their interests. You also need to spend time discussing children's interests with parents or carers. Planning the curriculum around the interests of the children will ensure that they are motivated, interested and engaged in the learning opportunities that you provide. Effective practitioners will use the children's interests as a starting point for developing and enhancing provision areas within their setting.

⊶ Key Point

- Spend time observing children's interests and try to take account of these in your planning.

Learning journeys

Throughout this text we refer to the use of learning journeys to document children's achievements. This approach allows practitioners to document evidence of learning in a range of ways, including the use of long and short observations, photographs, samples of children's recorded work, and discussions with parents and children. Children should be allowed to select some of the material that is included in the learning journey, and the voices of the parent and child should also be privileged and given pride of place within this record. Children, parents and all practitioners should be given free access to the learning journeys as well as being able to add information that they feel evidences significant achievement. Effective practitioners find ways of involving parents or carers with assessment and believe that the learning that takes place at home is as valuable as the learning that takes place inside the setting. The learning journey builds on the Reggio approach idea and challenges practitioners to document evidence of achievement in a range of ways in order to capture the multiplicity of ways through which children are able to express themselves.

Margaret Carr (2001) describes an approach called *learning stories*. According to Carr, learning stories 'are observations in everyday settings, designed to provide a cumulative series of qualitative "snapshots" or written vignettes of individual children' (Carr 2001: 96). Carr suggests that stories can be used to document children's attitudes and dispositions, such as levels of interest, being involved, persistence, ability to express an idea or a feeling, and taking responsibility or taking another point of view. Carr refers to these as *domains* (p96). The role of the practitioner in this approach is to document 'critical incidents' (Gettinger and Stoiber 1998) that highlight evidence of achievement within each of these domains. Children's stories can be kept in a portfolio and Carr suggests documenting the learning through the use of written narratives of critical incidents, photographs, copies of children's written work and drawings, and the use of comments from the children. Carr's approach offers real potential for collecting rich qualitative data about children's learning. It is possible that a learning story could evidence achievement in several domains, and Carr refers to this as *overlapping* (p97). It is likely that a child who is interested in a task will be more involved in the learning and thus this evidences achievement in two domains. Learning stories can include extracts of dialogue between children and should be easily accessible. Carr's approach requires practitioners to document learning within the domains over a range of contexts. Practitioners therefore need to be committed to observational assessment. Assessment in this model is seen as integral to teaching and learning, and not as a bolt-on. Practitioners need to have a secure understanding of each child's next steps in learning so that they capture the correct critical incidents.

O═━ Key Point

- Learning takes many forms and can be documented in a range of ways. Document children's learning through observations, photographs, samples of work, videos and audio recordings.

This chapter has reviewed key approaches to learning and teaching and the early years and has provided an overview of key learning theories. Ultimately, you will approach your practice with your own set of values and principles and these will shape your pedagogical approaches. All practitioners should be aware of different approaches to early years education and key theories. This will ensure that your personal philosophy of how children learn is informed, underpinned and therefore grounded.

Further Reading

Carr, M. (2001) *Assessment in Early Childhood Settings: Learning Stories*. London: SAGE.

- Chapter 6 is very useful as it includes information about the use of *learning stories* in assessment.

Cary, S. (2007) 'Reading the Signals: A Case Study Taken from Research on: Developing the Adult Role Within Children's Play', *Early Childhood Practice*, 9 (2): 50–63, for an application of the theoretical concept of 'metaplay'.

- The author of this case study is able to use detailed observations (and assessments) to 'bridge' children's thinking and play skills so that metaplay is nurtured alongside a growing awareness of the needs of others. This journal is an extremely accessible publication that includes a range of practitioner-led action research.

Hughes, A. M. (2006) *Developing Play for the Under Threes: The Treasure Basket and Heuristic Play*. London: David Fulton.

- This is an extremely effective handbook on how to practically organise heuristic play sessions and what to look for when making assessments of children's developing conceptual understanding.

Willan, J. (2004) 'Observing Children', in Willan, J., Parker-Rees, R. and Savage, J. (2004) *Early Childhood Studies.* Exeter: Learning Matters, (pp. 87–97).

- This is an accessible chapter on observing children that begins with Bronfenbrenner's view of the child living within a series of interconnected contexts, all of which impact on development. The theoretical perspective adopted by the observer (or assessor) is seen to have a distinct impact on what is seen as worth observing. Deciding what observations mean is also seen as being framed by the theoretical perspectives that we work with.

Yelland, N. (ed.) (2005) *Critical Issues in Early Childhood Education.* Maidenhead: Open University Press.

- For a wide-ranging series of challenges to some long-held beliefs in early childhood education. 'Critical' can be taken to mean crucial, and through a variety of authors you are encouraged to re-examine what is crucial or fundamental to your practice.

Useful Websites

www.unicef.org/crc/

- You can access the United Nations Convention on the Rights of the Child on this site.

www.educate.ece.govt.nz [accessed May 2009].

- 'A collaborative space where early childhood educators can share, reflect on and be inspired by quality teaching practice', and follow the links to Te Whariki, the New Zealand early childhood curriculum policy statement.

Values and principles of assessment in the Early Years Foundation Stage

Julie Percival

Chapter Objectives

- To consider why all practice begins with the careful consideration of values and principles.
- To reflect on current policy values and principles in relation to assessment.
- To assert the view that the Early Years Foundation Stage (EYFS) is a framework for regulation but also reflection, giving scope for autonomy.
- To consider how values and principles evolve over time: they are not fixed or given but shaped by our understanding.
- To prompt reflection and evaluation of assessment processes starting from shared principles.

Why is it important to include a chapter about values and principles in a book about assessment? Principles may be defined as a general set of rules or beliefs which guide behaviour. The EYFS (DCSF 2008c) themes and commitments have been the subject of information boards in the entrance halls of many early years settings. How many more focus instead on the six areas of learning, without reference to any underlying principles? Assessment is an integral part of practice and not an additional consideration once provision for care, learning and development has been decided upon. The values and principles you have adopted for your assessment practice should be in harmony with the values and principles that influence your wider work.

The policy context

The overarching aim of the *EYFS: Setting the Standards for Learning, Development and Care for Children from Birth to Five* (DCSF 2008) is to help children achieve the five *Every Child Matters* (DfES 2004) outcomes of staying safe, being healthy, enjoying and achieving, making a positive contribution, and achieving economic well-being. One of the ways in which the policymakers hope this will happen is through the setting of universal standards that all providers of childcare and early education can refer to as a basis for their work. These standards should offer parents reassurance and enable workers across the variety of provision to have a shared professional language. Most importantly, entitlement to quality should not to be dependent on where children live, their ethnicity, culture or religion, home language, family background, learning needs or disabilities, gender or ability.

The commitment to improve the lives of children and young people has been reinforced with the publication of *The Children's Plan: Building Brighter Futures* (DCSF 2007). The theme of this document is that 'services do not bring children up, parents do.' Collaborative respectful partnerships between practitioners, children and families should be a feature of universal services and ensure that in times of need, children are supported to have the best possible outcomes. For responsive, flexible services to be a reality, practitioners must hold certain principles and values in the forefront of their mind. This can be quite challenging.

Both *Every Child Matters* (DfES 2004) and the *Children's Plan* (DCSF 2007) are the focal point for a plethora of initiatives and guidelines. It is not altogether clear how the values and principles will be translated into effective practice. Each layer of decision making must grapple with the values and principles contained within the documents, knowledge of existing resources, and histories of service delivery – along with local and practitioner priorities.

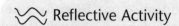 Reflective Activity

Visit the following sites to find out more about two useful documents that you can use to develop your thinking.

- Go to www.info4localgov.uk to find the General Social Care Council (2008) Values for Integrated Working with Children and Young People.

  o   What kind of practitioners do children value?
  o   What key attributes underpin values-led practice?
  o   Within your particular specialism and through integrated working, it is suggested that the values shown in Table 2.1 should underpin practice.

Table 2.1   Aspects of professional practice that exemplify value-led practice

respect	trustworthiness	patience
honesty	reliability	integrity
resilience	supportive	sensitivity
transparency	positive	creativity
listen and take account	clear communication	safeguarding

Could you define these values? Could you cite an example of your practice that exemplifies each value?

- Go to www.everychildmatters.gov.uk/ to find the Common Core of Skills and Knowledge for the Children's Workforce (DfES 2005). Within the Common Core prospectus, communication is seen as central to working with children, young people, and their families and carers.

  o   How do your behaviour and your everyday practice communicate your values?
  o   Trust, rapport, continuity and engagement underpin effective communication. What do you understand by these terms? Do you think there is a shared understanding, common to the practitioners you work alongside?
  o   How can you evidence your thoughts?

The EYFS: designed for reflection

The *EYFS: Setting the Standards for Learning, Development and Care for Children from Birth to Five* is a collection of documents that is made up of five elements. The *Statutory Framework* (DCSF 2008a) sets out the legal requirements relating to welfare, learning and development. The *Practice Guidance* (DCSF 2008b) contains 'essential advice and guidance' for those working with babies, toddlers and young children, from birth until the term after they are 5 years old. There is a pack of 24 *Principles into Practice Cards* (DCSF 2008c) that are designed to be a source of 'best practice'. The *Wall Poster* serves as a 'daily reminder' of some of the needs of children and the principles of the EYFS. Finally, the CD-ROM contains all four documents along with an extensive bank of information and resources.

The EYFS pack (DCSF 2008) seems to have been designed to help front-line practitioners develop practice in particular kinds of ways. All do need to be clear about the basic minimum standards that enable provision to be operational and registered with Ofsted, but this is not all that is offered. Examples of best practice and research are accessible, with a commitment to the updating of the online resource index. Questions to prompt reflection are posed on the cards. Principles are mapped out for all to see. The EYFS became mandatory in September 2008. However, there remains considerable flexibility and choice as to how you use this pack to respond to the uniqueness of each child. Relationships and environments evolve according to the decisions you make. Children's creativity and enthusiasm, confidence, and sense of self-worth are in your hands. How have you chosen to work with the principles?

- Which document from the pack has had the most use in your setting?

- If our practice is a reflection of our values, what does your *use* of the EYFS materials show about your approach to supporting the care, learning and development of young children?

Accountability: a reflective approach to regulations

The implementation of the EYFS is monitored and inspected by Ofsted through a process that begins with completing a self-evaluation form designed around the EYFS statutory requirements and the *Every Child Matters* outcomes. Rules and regulations have long been a feature of working with babies, toddlers and young children. Prior to the introduction of the EYFS in September 2008, the *National Standards for Under 8s Day Care and Childminding* (DfES 2003), the *Birth to Three Matters Framework* (DfES 2002), and the *Curriculum Guidance for the Foundation Stage* (DfES 2000) were used to structure and guide practice. The previous inspection regime for private, voluntary and independent settings (such as private day nurseries, playgroups and independent schools) was based on the

Every Child Matters outcomes and reflective, evidence-based practice was implied.

Currently, practitioners are requested, for example to 'take a critical look at the effectiveness of what you and any assistants or staff do to help children enjoy learning and achieve as much as they can' (Ofsted 2008). Evidence of the impact of practice needs to be recorded along with any plans for improvement. The views of stake-holders, as with any inspection, have to be recorded. It is not enough to have, for example, the appropriate number of practitioners employed, or the appropriate policies in place: in the spirit of the EYFS, practitioners should be working reflectively for quality and equality. This involves each lead practitioner having an understanding of what is being done, when and how, along with why certain prac-tices take place and what the impact of those practices are.

Deciding 'what next', either session by session or through the setting of longer-term goals, requires careful thought. Why choose this course of action? Will stakeholders be consulted? What resources are required? What techniques and behaviours will be important? What will success look like?

The EYFS can be a source of support to help teams to discuss their values and make choices about their practice. Fundamentally, set-tings and their teams – including you as an individual – are being asked to be accountable for the quality of what you provide. More cynically, you are being asked to account to the taxpayer for any funding, such as Nursery Education Funding or Graduate Leader Fund, that you receive. Are you spending wisely? Accountability is part of professional responsibility.

Families access care outside their own home for their children for very many reasons. They send their children to school, again, for many reasons. To date, rules and regulations have not eliminated the diversity of provision available to children and parents, nor have they led to uniformly good (or, indeed, excellent) provision.

Communicating clearly and purposefully about your work could be seen as a fundamental responsibility. It enables you to demonstrate the basis upon which you do indeed put children at the centre of what you do and practically how it is done. Without a certain amount of evidence gathering, reflection, action and review, could you be certain that you were not basing decisions on personal assumptions and intuition? Reflective processes can also help target driven settings to complement numerical data with richer qualitative data that are more accessible to a wider range of audiences, such as parents and children. Reflect on your values, the aspects of your work you believe are vital for young children to thrive, and the guiding principles that you return to when you need inspiration or support to make a decision. Regulations provide a framework but regulations are open to interpretation. How regulations are played out in your setting is to a large extent in your hands.

Finding a theoretical grounding for your work

Values and principles can be hidden in our beliefs about the children in our care. Along with our personal assumptions and intuition, we are offered a variety of theoretical perspectives upon which to base our decision making and evidence gathering. MacNaughton (2003) challenges practitioners to think critically about their ideas and methods so that they can account for their practice both to themselves and others. Different theoretical positions are grouped according to their fundamental view of the child as a being but also a learner. Table 2.2 has been created through the selection of just one example of a position that sits within each of the three paradigms. When you look out onto the children and the setting you work in, what you see and attend to is mediated by the theories you subscribe to. This in turn impacts on how you assess children and make provision for their well-being and learning.

Table 2.2   Comparing theoretical positions, their implicit values and principles

Child	Practitioner	Assessment
'Conforming' position (e.g. behaviourism) Culture determines learning: behaviour is shaped so that children can conform.		
Starts off unknowing, uninitiated, liable to become bored. Compliant, ready and willing to learn if appropriately motivated, the rules are clear and the rewards/sanctions consistently applied.	Direct the learning through carefully designed programmes with clearly stated goals that can be monitored and measured. Refine, remodel and prepare the child to 'fit in'.	Measures what has been taught, perhaps to the exclusion of other aspects of development and learning. Assessment tasks are designed to complement the instructional programme and can be standardised across all learners. Accountability comes through standardisation and measurability?

Table 2.2   (Continued)

Child	Practitioner	Assessment
'Reforming' position (e.g. constructivism) The interaction between nature and culture enables thinking to be reformed and improved as the child progresses through stages in development.		
Learns through the senses as a social being. Builds own understanding but this can be shaped by interaction with and through the physical and social environment. Competent at each stage of development with the propensity to see themselves as active learners.	Carefully design the environment so that children can learn by doing, using open-ended materials and play. Focus on intellectual performance as an indicator of holistic well-being. Facilitate creative thinking. Learning possibilities are identified.	Observes and reflects on how the child operates in the environment (context) provided. Assessment systems are designed to capture the child's interests and dispositions along with the learning process, not just the end product. Curriculum development and assessment opportunities are interwoven and evolve. Accountability comes through the practitioner knowledge of developmental ages and stages and/or the prevailing national policy framework.
'Transforming' position (e.g. postmodern, social constructionalism) Learning can only be understood within and through the context in which it occurs. Understanding and relationships are transformed or reconstructed through situated interaction.		
Development implies the child is less formed than an adult, instead the child is seen as a meaning maker, a contributor and influencer from birth. Learning takes place in and through race, gender and class. As social beings, the collective learning is as relevant as the personal learning.	Attention is paid to the values and power relations. Differences are not only acknowledged but explored because learning is 'situated' in different places and times. Planning centres on equity and what is just, and is based on the dynamics of the group as well as children's interests and the collaboratively constructed curriculum.	Is a process shared between practitioners, parents and carers and the child. Responsibility is taken to ensure that the assessment systems. capture how children learn in and through their culture, gender race and disability. Ages and stages (norms) are seen as cultural tools with a limited use for some settings. Accountability comes through: • active participation, the documentation and relationships of those involved; • the application of detailed knowledge of pedagogy across a range of domains of care learning and development along with the prevailing national policy framework.

Source: adapted from MacNaughton 2003.

Being accountable for our practice in an autonomous, professional way relies on being able to identify the source of our beliefs about children, families and our practice. At times we need to challenge our beliefs, discuss them openly, and maybe alter the course of our actions. We need to acknowledge that there are multiple ways of viewing children, but also that children have multiple ways of being themselves.

The EYFS CD-ROM is a well-researched collection of ideas, carefully selected on the basis of growing theoretical knowledge and understanding of a variety of aspects of early years work. It is possible to interpret the inclusion of this resource in the pack as an attempt to take the information to the practitioners in the hope that theoretical concepts and suggestions for effective practice will be more widely disseminated. Perhaps practitioners will be reminded of key concepts covered during initial training? Perhaps leaders and managers will structure time into the working week for professional discussion?

'There's no time for values and principles and besides the EYFS is more or less the same as the other documents it replaced'

Unfortunately, evidence of what has worked before, reported outcomes of carefully designed research and accessible interpretations of theory, can easily be left on the bookshelf. The learning and development grids that look quite like the stepping stones from the Curriculum Guidance for the Foundation Stage (DfES 2000) could be well thumbed. On a weekly basis, practitioners may become more familiar with the grids as they match observations to 'Look, listen and note' statements.

Superficially at least, it seems that the EYFS is being implemented. Unfortunately, without taking the time to consider the values that underpin practice, the following two dangers (at least) may occur:

1. A system is grafted onto existing practice. Confident practitioners, familiar with their effective routines, care practices and rich curriculum, may lose momentum. There are a variety of reasons why they have not been able to reflect on their wealth of skill and knowledge. They have strong values yet these are not clearly articulated: they are not readily to mind to be integrated with new

ideas. This loss of momentum can be disheartening. Less effective practitioners begin to appreciate the need for development so systems and processes are adopted quickly. Some practitioners are not sure why new systems need to be put in place. Without the underpinning rationale, setbacks cannot be explained – the vision cannot be defended. The EYFS becomes just another policy direc- tive that has been found wanting. For some there is a strong feeling that once again they could not match up to the expecta- tions placed upon them. For others, the explanation that policy- makers never really know about the 'real world experiences' of working with young children seems plausible.

2. Practice remains the same (but with different headings on the planning sheet!). Policies say children are at the heart of practice, but practice does not bear this out. The 'folk model' of practice described by Margaret Carr (2007) is perpetuated through the common-sense, gut instinct approach. Values and principles are never explored. Institutionalised, 'one-size-fits-all' routines con- tinue to dehumanise children. Inappropriate learning experiences are repeated and dispositions to explore and solve problems whither. Practitioners know what to do when required. A principled approach to practice passes the setting by.

Values and principles: themes and commitments

The four principles of the EYFS are:

- Every child is a competent learner from birth who can be resilient, capable, confident and self-assured, the *theme* of this principle being the uniqueness of the child.

- Children learn to be strong and independent from a base of loving and secure relationships with parents and/or a key person: the *theme* of this principle is positive relationships.

- The environment plays a key role in supporting and extending children's development and learning: the *theme* of this principle is enabling environments.

- Children develop and learn in different ways and at different rates, and all areas of learning and development are equally impor- tant and interconnected: children's learning and development are the *themes* of this principle.

Table 2.3   The underpinning values of integrated working and the EYFS commitments

Respect for each human being's capacities and their culture. No child or family is discriminated against	**Trustworthiness** You trust each child to be themselves: they trust you to be genuine and loving	**Patience** Environments, development, learning and relationships do not happen overnight
Honesty Fundamental to building a secure and loving relationship together	**Reliability** Fundamental to building a secure and loving relationship together	**Integrity** Fundamental to building a secure and loving relationship together
Resilience Work with young children is varied, complex, challenging and rewarding! Promoting resilience in children and colleagues enables us to face the challenges of life	**Supportive** Development and learning can be challenging; all children need to build confidence in their abilities – supportive relationships with adults who are generous with their knowledge beat any amount of resources	**Sensitivity** Intimate and personal care carried out sensitively on the basis of a careful review of need is the basis of all work with babies and young children. Sensing when to support children's learning – using your senses in combination with knowledge
Transparency Openness supports secure relationships with babies, children, parents, colleagues and the wider community of professionals – agendas are not hidden – testing does not masquerade as play	**Positive** Enables you to constructively build relationships and environments where children can be seen as capable	**Creativity** Using every resource to flexibly respond to the child's needs and interests Being open to possibilities, different patterns of need and learning, that adult's knowledge can be used flexibly/creatively to meet needs and take learning further
Listen and take account *Time* is made for children, parents and colleagues to express their view, and the environment, care plans and provision for learning reflects this	**Clear communication** Ambiguity is kept to a minimum. Children know they are loved and valued; they know what they are good at and that communication is a two-way process	**Safeguarding** Every child (every person) is potentially vulnerable. Psychological and physical well-being is central for children to become resilient adults

Direct links between the values set out for integrated working and the principles of the EYFS (DCSF 2008) have been made in Table 2.3.

What do these values and principles look like in everyday practice? Given the diversity of the sector, it is only to be expected that they will look different in every setting! The EYFS in some respects is a 'manifesto' of beliefs laid out under the four themes. Working to any principles requires a *commitment* to certain beliefs about children and best practice. There are four commitments for each of the four themes. If you have made a commitment to work in a certain way, try to understand why this might be. If you are studying for a qualification, you are probably using a learning journal to help you reflect on the content of the course and its application to your work-based learning. Mind mapping or simply writing can be a useful starting point for reflection. If you are not sure what you are committed to, now is a good time to get deciding!

A principled approach to practice is not new

Bruce's influential text (1987, first edition) argued for a principled approach to practice that could empower practitioners in their decision making. Table 2.4 compares Bruce's principles with a more recent publication from the series edited by Hurst and Joseph (Brooker 2008). Decades have gone by. Priorities change or are expressed in new ways, and notions of what constitutes quality practice evolve over time.

The highly regarded approach to supporting and documenting children's learning that has been developed by the teams who work in the Reggio Emilia region of Italy is founded on what Rinaldi calls 'a sensitivity to knowledge' (2006: 72) and a richness of questioning. The 'pedagogy of listening' (Rinaldi 2006: 65) helps practitioners to be curious and doubtful, to suspend prejudice and be open to change. A series of values and principles do not provide answers but they do provide an evolving framework for learning about practice, which in turn informs our decision making. The EYFS principles have evolved through the accumulated thinking, provoked by key thinkers (of which Bruce, Brooker, Hurst and Joseph cited here are examples) and the lobbying of practitioners and researchers. In many ways they represent compromise between a host of competing policymaking agendas. However, they do provide space for you to reflect and take ownership of your work; to exercise your senses, to represent not only the thinking of children but also the hundred, if

Table 2.4 Changing principles over time

Ten common principles of early childhood education	Principles for a developmental curriculum
• Childhood is seen as valid in itself, as part of life, and not simply as a preparation for adulthood. • The whole child is considered important. • Learning is not compartmentalised into subject areas. • Child-initiated, self-directed activity is valued because it is an indication of the child's motivation to explore. • Nurture self-discipline. • Receptive periods are characterised by patterns in behaviour that support learning and exploration (such as schemas). • What children can do (rather than what they cannot) is considered first when assessing and planning for the future. • Favourable conditions support children to display their thinking and connect their inner life with the world around them. • Interaction with peers and adults is of central importance. • 'Education is seen as an interaction between the child and the environment, including in particular, other people and knowledge itself.'	• Each child is an individual and should be respected and treated as such. • The early years is a specialism with its own criteria of appropriate practice. • Support for young children centres on their concerns and actively engages them. • The practitioner has the responsibility to counter negative messages and foster positive attitudes. • 'Each child's cultural and linguistic endowment is seen as the fundamental medium of learning.' • Anti-discriminatory approaches are essential for a developmentally appropriate curriculum. • 'All children should be offered opportunities to progress and develop and should have equal access to good quality provision.' • Coherence and continuity in the offered and experienced curriculum is founded on partnership with parents. • Quality provision is linked to democratic relationships.
From Bruce, T. (1987) *Early Childhood Education.* London: Hodder Stoughton (p10).	From Brooker, L. (2008) *Supporting Transitions in the Early Years.* Supporting Early Learning Series. Maidenhead: Open University Press (pp. ix–x).

not the thousand languages, symbols and codes we use when we carry out our work.

Energy and time are necessary but the journey is worth beginning. Your values and principles will evolve, and the way your practice is framed by them will almost certainly never stay the same as each child comes into the setting, each policy imperative looms, or, most importantly, your own understanding or 'sensitivity to knowledge' (Rinaldi 2006) blossoms.

O— Key Point

- Audit where you are before making changes to practice. Incremental (or even whole-scale) changes without reference back to principles and values can lead to disjointed practice: sometimes it seems expedient to do something and yet on reflection it takes you off course (Table 2.5).

Table 2.5   Interrogating our assessment of young children: an audit

Assessing young children's care, learning and development

Question and describe
Who will contribute to this description? Children, families, colleagues?
What is being done to inform our understanding of the child?
When are assessments taking place?
How are assessments being carried out?
What aspects of care, learning and development are assessed?
How is information gained and used?

Question and evaluate
What is the quality of the assessment information we gather?
Have we decided on a rationale for our judgements about quality?
What is the impact of our assessment processes on children?
What is the impact of our assessment processes on families?
What is the impact of our assessment processes on colleagues?

Question and analyse
Why does assessment happen the way that it does?
How are decisions about the assessment processes made?
Whose voice is heard loudest – child, parent or practitioner?
Do our assessments actually have a positive (or negative) impact on our systems, routines and provision?
Can we see our values and principles/the EYFS principles in our work?
If yes, can we document this and celebrate it?
If no, can we begin a process of development so that the uniqueness of the child is supported through responsive relationship and enabling environments?
How will we document our shared learning: children and adults together?

Mary Jane Drummond (2003) has been involved with supporting early years workers to reflect on their practice for many years. Assessment practice can be challenging and a worry for adults and children alike, depending on the type of assessment tools being used. Her experience, supported by her research leads her to assert that

Effective assessment – clear seeing, rich understanding, respectful application – will be advanced by a full appreciation of the value-base from which teachers' choices are made. (Drummond 2003: 14)

Having gathered the data for your audit, you should ensure you have time to *read* and *interpret* and then *recall* and *reconstruct* your understanding (Rinaldi 2006). What activities attract the most time and effort? How do the most time-consuming activities inform your understanding of each child's learning? Are the assessment activities enabling the enriching of the learning experience for each and every child?

The concept of the work-based learner-practitioner (Rawlings 2008) working within a 'community of practice' (Lave and Wenger 1998) is a useful one for all interested in assessing children and provision. Article 12 of the UN Convention on the Rights of the Child encourages adults to ensure that children actively contribute to decision making where matters concern them. Their views should be taken seriously and the child's competent participation should be expected and nurtured (Clarke and Moss 2001; Lancaster and Broadbent 2005). It takes a particular type of listening and a challenging of certain discourses to consider alternative perspectives. The audit is a suggested starting point for understanding what is actually happening in your setting. Definitive answers as to what and how to assess cannot be supplied to fit the needs of every setting. Learning together, building shared understandings, and revisiting actual actions in the light of values and principles can help to keep coherence and quality at the forefront of your practice.

Purposeful assessment

The purposes of your assessment practice must be kept in mind and balanced carefully so that one purpose does not outweigh another. Nutbrown (2006), for example, identifies three broad purposes:

- Assessment for management and accountability.

- Assessment for research.

- Assessment for teaching and learning.

Implicit in this list of purposes is the need for practitioners to ensure that well-being is accounted for and built into any setting's practice. We assess to ensure equity of practice and delivery of social policy imperatives. We assess to find out more about our practice and its impact on all involved. We assess to celebrate children's learning and so practitioners can select what they might teach next and how they might teach it.

However, the EYFS does not just provide a framework for practice in schools. For many practitioners the intimate care of groups of children must be carefully thought out and organised for extended periods of the day. Children's well-being is a feature of much unrecognised practice in terms of assessment in the EYFS.

> Care was (and to many still is) regarded as second best to education and this tunnel vision has been a serious obstacle in the way of quality provision for very young children. (Lindon 2006: 23)

Tuning to children's sleep patterns or preferences for being comforted and changed, for example, is a vital consideration for many parents and carers but also early years practitioners. It is not that schools do not provide a caring environment – they most certainly do! Practitioners throughout the EYFS should to be open to the need to assess children's well-being so that they can plan appropriately for care that respects each child as an individual. Supporting babies and young children in their development in ways that respond to individual patterns in growth and development takes careful observation and the application of high levels of knowledge and skill. Routines must be carefully planned to ensure that dehumanising systems do not evolve and that each person living in a care-led setting feels first and foremost respected as a person, not just a learner, capable of achieving the Early Learning Goals.

Alongside assessment for teaching and learning should come assessment for care and well-being. Progress that is trackable through the 'learning and development grids' (DCSF 2008b) should be interlinked with a child's fundamental well-being. This is not a plea for additional, specialised assessment techniques, but a valuing of the social, interpersonal assessment that many practitioners carry out and use to inform their daily practice. Closely linked to a child's learning, assessment for care and well-being needs asserting as valuable and purposeful in its own right.

Owning values and principles

Read the following case study. It illustrates how a group of practitioners chose to learn about their own practice so that they could improve their assessment of children's behaviour. They used their beliefs about children and the principles of the EYFS to help guide their choices as to how their practice needed to develop.

 Case Study: a team explore their values and principles, as they search for a way to change practice

An early years professional (EYP) working alongside a team of colleagues discussed how the behaviour of some children was causing concern. Their informal assessments had not been transferred to written observations, as generally, those were only made for significant achievements within the six areas of learning (DCSF 2008a). Negative behaviour was not really something they chose to record, unless part of a particular strategy for particularly inappropriate behaviour. Lots of instances of inappropriate behaviour seemed to be occurring. Various ideas were floated as to how to deal with the situation. The only consensus was that something had to change so that things could settle down again and parents would not feel there was a problem.

The EYP decided to lead a staff meeting, using the work of Louise Porter (2003) to help the team step back from the behaviour and talk about their values and principles (Table 2.6).

There were some very challenging discussions, as the staff were asked to place themselves along the continuum between controlling and guiding children in their learning about their behaviour. Assessments of behaviour were coloured by the views practitioners held about children, their behaviour, and the possible intervention methods. The discussion about rewards and punishments became particularly heated!

When they looked at principles of the EYFS, alongside the work of Porter (2003), it seemed as if they should reconsider their assessment of their children's behaviour. It was decided to follow the current setting policy for the time being, but to jot down instances of the behaviour that caused concern to review at the next meeting.

The team spent 2 weeks making brief observations of instances of behaviour they deemed inappropriate and sharing some short sections from the EYFS and other literature: this gave them some thinking space so that when they met again, they were ready to reflect on values and principles, and consider what the behaviour consisted of and why it might be happening. Their assessments of the children led them to reconsider their provision, but, significantly, they began to formulate some different strategies for responding to children's behaviour, based on the principles behind the guidance style of discipline.

During subsequent meetings colleagues confided that they found it really difficult to work in a guiding way. Sometimes it was more time-consuming and needed such patience! They juggled with making sure that children knew what was unacceptable or hurtful and remaining calm, when sometimes behaviour seemed very challenging.

For the next 6 months, behaviour became a standing item on the agenda. By then the EYP felt able to review the behaviour management policy. The staff decided that the policy needed a new title that reflected the new approaches being taken. Words like control and management were replaced in the document with support and guidance. Staff responded to the unique learning needs of the child through their key person system and talked with parents about their work. They built in time to explore powerful emotions rather than push them to one side. Talking explicitly with children about feelings became an accepted aspect of their work that warranted time, resources, recording and assessment – the curriculum became enriched and assessments acknowledged children's emotional intelligence. The environment became more settled. Values and principles led the development of practice.

Drummond (2003) argues that claiming principles as your own will not bring about the changes that you hope for. She discusses how thinking about practice should be scaffolded so that answers do not come from a policy document with principles, an authoritative text (such as Porter's), or set behaviour management techniques derived from psychological theory (for example, reward systems such as sticker charts). These can only be starting points to prompt thinking. The confidence of the practitioners to make changes in their assessment of behaviour in this case study came from their questioning of what was going on and how it related to their values and principles. This questioning of what is good and worthwhile is central to our autonomy as professionals.

Table 2.6   A continuum of styles of discipline: a copy of the handout that was discussed

Control ◄——— Discipline style ———► Guidance		
Lies *outside* the child: control is in the hands of the 'rule-maker'	**Locus of control**	Lies *within* the child: the child is supported to exercise control over their own behaviour
Obedience and compliance are prioritised through direct instruction Challenging feelings need to be controlled or ignored, not acknowledged and explored	**Goals**	Strategies are used by adults to support children to • be autonomously considerate • develop ways of dealing with (powerful) emotions • cooperate with those around them • have a sense that they too have an impact on the community/ setting in which they live
Perhaps adults have failed to 'reward' appropriate behaviour sufficiently Perhaps inappropriate behaviour has been inadvertently rewarded or gone unchecked	**Causes of disruptive behaviour**	Normal exuberance Normal exploration Lack of coordination and or self-control Natural response to having little autonomy or chance to learn about feelings and actions
It is natural for all children to misbehave Sometimes children are 'naughty'	**View of children**	Children learn to 'behave' at different rates and in different ways Will behave well if treated well
Inappropriate Wilful noncompliance	**View of disruptive behaviour**	An opportunity for scaffolding the learning Some errors are inevitable – we all wish we could have done things differently sometimes!
Rewards Punishments	**Intervention methods**	Acknowledgement (not necessarily agreement!) Problem solving and resolution
Dictator!	**Adult status**	Emotionally intelligent leader

(Source: adapted from Porter, 2003, p18).

Assessment as your opportunity to learn

The questioning was not a comfortable process for the practitioners in the case study. Carr (2007) describes how she was anxious to be seen as the competent practitioner in the face of her local community and the parents. She assumed that readiness for school was the main priority for her and her children in terms of assessment (and in turn for her planning of the curriculum). Niggled by the fact that exciting learning episodes were going unrecognised, she decided to challenge her assumptions and reviewed her assessment practice. The documenting of children's learning that Carr and her colleaques developed has been very well received. The 'learning stories' are purposeful and identify the focus for future interventions for the practitioner, parent and child together. Progression can be seen and authenticity is captured so that parents and children can connect with the learning – it means something to them and they develop the language of learning for themselves, so that they can join in the talk that surrounds assessment. Administrative demands are met through tracking sheets. But the tracking sheets do not stand alone – evidence supports the ticks and highlighted sections. Children are not seen as one-dimensional, following a single pathway because the time and effort goes proportionately into the stories and not just the tracking.

Rights and responsibilities

Value the time you spend exploring your values and principles! You have the right to work in an environment where all are prepared to challenge ideas and existing practice. You have the right make choices about practice. You have the right to have your values acknowledged.

But with your rights, you have responsibilities. When you challenge ideas and practice, you have a responsibility to have a reasoned, researched position. You are responsible for choosing to practise in a way that puts the child at the centre of what you do. You are responsible for implementing the statutory requirements of the EYFS. However, approaching the implementation of the EYFS as a practitioner-learner (Rawlings 2008) with integrity will give you scope for expressing your values and keeping them with you as you work.

Provision for young children in the EYFS must address well-being and learning. Assessments will never be worthy of the child if they do not take account of the powerful and varied ways children influence their world and learn through it. If provision is narrow and unresponsive, assessments will only reveal a partial picture. Accountability, a worry for many practitioners will remain elusive. Reviewing your principles and checking that they drive your decision making can put the child at the centre of your work and in turn ensure that assessments are useful and authentic.

Further Reading

Both the Clarke and Moss (2001) text and the Lancaster and Broadbent (2005) (see references) materials provide practitioners and parents and carers with underpinning knowledge and practice skills to aid listening to children. Suggestions for 'when', 'why' and 'how' to listen are skilfully woven together, making for inspirational reading.

Fleer, M. (2006) 'The Cultural Construction of Child Development: Creating Institutional and Cultural Intersubjectivity', *International Journal of Early Years Education*, 14 (2): 127–140.

- This is a theoretical paper that asks readers to broaden their assumptions about institutionalised practice so that they can better understand children in the context in which they live. This will lead you to consider the work of Lave and Wenger.

Marsh, J. ed. (2005) *Popular Culture, New Media and Digital Literacy in Early Childhood*. London: Routledge Falmer.

- This locates children, with their multiple identities, as competent learners within their culture. The gap between home-based learning and setting-based experiences of new media challenges the possible misconception that the setting is the place where children learn. Our assessments are incomplete when we fail to acknowledge the cultural world in which and through which children learn.

Penn, H. (2008) *Understanding Early Childhood: Issues and Controversies*. Maidenhead: McGraw-Hill/Open University Press.

- Accessible problematising of taken-for-granted understandings and practice, including consideration of the ethics of routine observation (or surveillance) of children.

Seitz, H. and Bartholomew, C. (2008) 'Powerful Portfolios for Young Children', *International Journal of Early Years Education*, 36 (1): 63–68.

- This article makes the case for 'authentic assessments' through portfolios that are constructed by the child, the parent and the practitioner. However, from the start there are clear lines of responsibility for each partner, and time is planned for all to share in the assessment process. The lasting meaningful documentation enables parents and children to understand the learning process more fully and for practitioners to take responsibility for identifying relevant national benchmarks for accountability purposes.

Whalley, M. and the Penn Green Centre Team (2007) *Involving Parents in Their Children's Learning,* 2nd edn. London: Paul Chapman.

- Each person who goes through the doors of this centre for children and families is seen as having the capacity to be self-directing and capable of 'constructive discontent' (Whalley 2007). Are parents viewed as having a reasoned voice that you take account of?

Useful Websites

www.info4localgov.uk/documents/publications [accessed May 2008].

- General Social Care Council (2008) *Values for Integrated Working with Children and Young People.*

www.ofsted.gov.uk/Ofsted-home/Forms-and-guidance [accessed May 2008].

- Office for Standards in Education (Ofsted) (no date) *Early Years Self Evaluation Form and Guidance.*

www.ofsted.gov.uk/Ofsted-home/Forms-and-guidance [accessed May 2008].

- Office for Standards in Education (Ofsted) (no date) *Are You Ready for Your Inspection? A Guide to Inspection of Provision on Ofsted's Childcare and Early Years Registers.*

www.standards.dfes.gov.uk/eyfs/ [accessed May 2008].

- Department for Children, Schools and Families (DCSF) (2008) *The Early Years Foundation Stage: Setting Standards for Learning Development and Care for Children from Birth to Five.* Nottingham: DCSF.

www.ewenger.com/theory/ [accessed May 2009].

- Wenger, E. (no date) *Communities of Production: A Brief Introduction.*

3

Enabling environments

Denise Chadwick and Anne Webster

Chapter Objectives

- To consider features that contribute to a 'quality early years environment' and understand how it can be organised, both indoors and out, to support and challenge pupil learning.
- To share ideas how early years practitioners meet the needs of all children, by ongoing assessment of children's skills and holistic development to plan for challenging future experiences.

This chapter will explore the kind of learning experiences and environment that practitioners provide in order to create quality early years provision. It will challenge you to think about not only the experiences you plan for children in your care but also the importance of supporting their well-being and making opportunity for themselves and their family in their ongoing learning and development. The importance of working closely with parents and carers will be considered as an important link in meeting the needs of individuals. The thoughts of Vygotsky, Froebel and Isaacs will be discussed as we consider the messages in the Early Years Foundation Stage (EYFS) about how children learn best through an appropriate balance of adult- and child-led play experiences.

The early years teaching and learning environment

The environment should be exciting to children, inspiring them to explore and learn. It needs to support their individual stage of development and offer challenge across all six areas of learning as defined in the new EYFS framework. You need to make sure that you are offering children a carefully planned, well-balanced and organised learning environment that offers access to learning challenges, building on earlier experiences and enabling them to make good progress from their own unique starting point.

The physical characteristics of any environment can ultimately influence the overall design and will often determine the kinds of choices that are made. For example, if an indoor environment has limited floor space, it will obviously impact upon the number of areas that you can offer on a daily basis. You need to ensure, however, that the daily provision covers the basic curriculum as defined within the EYFS, and that the learning environment is regularly enhanced to develop and extend children's learning.

The EYFS is very clear in its explanation of the importance of both indoor and outdoor learning and how children need to be given regular access to outdoor learning experiences. Bilton (1998) identified 10 guiding principles for working in what she called the 'outdoor classroom' and clearly explained that the success of an outdoor environment is often dependent on adults' enthusiasm for it. However, outdoor play is central to young children's learning. Depending on children's individual styles, outdoor learning may be more valuable to some children than others; therefore, it is essential that practitioners give it equal priority. Adults need to carefully plan daily opportunities for learning and exploration in a well-managed, secure and safe outdoor environment. Opportunities should be made to interact with children's play, and it is the responsibility of the adults to bring the learning in the two environments together. Vygotsky believed that it was the quality of such interaction that allows children to function at a higher level (Vygotsky 1978).

Organising the environment to maximise opportunity for learning

The environment needs to be organised in different ways to offer inclusive practice. You need to be flexible when planning continuous provision areas and consider how children will access the resources and their individual level of physical skills. Does the opportunity to enter into a painting activity have to be made at an easel only? What is wrong in providing a similar opportunity on the floor with cushions for easier sitting and support for those children who enjoy applying paint in this dimension, and may not yet have mastered the skill of successfully applying paint from a pot to a vertical surface? Why not take the painting experience to a large-scale project in the outdoor area, substituting small brushes for household paintbrushes and rollers, and taking this learning to a new dimension. This allows greater opportunity for gross motor movements, which may be more appropriate to their current level of skill. It is therefore important that you consider the process of the activity and give equal attention as to the intended outcome.

Are you allowing children to be successful learners and practice skills or are you minimising their opportunity to do so? Reflective practitioners continually evaluate their practice and take children's individual learning and development needs into consideration.

Encouraging independence in children at this early stage of learning is essential, and one way this can be achieved is in the way resources are presented to them. An example of this is shown in Figure 3.1, as children are encouraged to choose daily activities, which can then be displayed in a pictorial timetable to support their learning. As each activity is completed, children remove the appropriate illustration and insert it in the pocket at the bottom of the chart. Thus, adults can see quickly those children who may fail to engage in learning tasks, and children have a clear understanding of their daily learning challenges.

Ideally, furniture should be child height so children can gain easy access to labelled resources and return them efficiently with the same degree of independence and responsibility. The 'high-scope' approach to learning, which has its origins in the USA, promotes child-led learning environments, using furniture that adheres to specific child-height dimensions. This approach to early years challenges children to make choices for learning and includes pictorial timetables for all children who access resources from purposely designed furniture and storage areas.

To encourage both independent and social learning play experiences, settings are usually organised into a number of areas and appropriate resources are introduced that allow children to practise skills and explore new avenues of learning and understanding.

Figure 3.1   Pictorial timetable

A typical list of areas although not exhaustive would be:

- Role-play or structured play areas.

- Literacy or mark-making area.

- Creative or messy area.

- Sand play; both wet and dry.

- Water area.

- Book and reading/story area.

- Numeracy and problem-solving area.

- ICT and exploratory area.

- Carpet area.

- Investigative area.

- Outdoor provision.

How to organise and where to site such areas needs careful forward planning. As suggested earlier in this chapter, specific features of the individual settings, such as floor space, access to bathroom and washing facilities, and entrance and exit points to outdoors, are typical examples that influence the choices for the final design. There are certain matters of logistics, however, that do need to be addressed as you begin to plan and organise your environment in order to present effective learning opportunities:

- Do the messy play provision areas have access to water and a suitable washable floor surface to meet safety requirements and not limit exploratory creative play?

- Is the quiet, reading book area in a place that is away from a thoroughfare to avoid unnecessary disturbance and noise that could interfere with children's ability to engage?

- Are you making the most of opportunities for using display to support children's learning? (Look at wall space, pinboards, radiators, etc.)

- Have you a carpeted area large enough to comfortably seat the whole group at any one time and offer opportunity for adult-led activity?

- Is there easy access to the outdoor provision area and can children and adults move freely and safely in and out of the two areas?

Along with busy areas of provision providing opportunity for active play and exploration, children also need quiet areas and a place to withdraw in solitude should they wish. Like adults, they, too, need time to experience a calm environment that offers them a slowing down of pace in a busy day. Music, lighting and comfortable seating add to the ambience of such areas and provide a meaningful and enjoyable place for children to withdraw, either independently or with adult support. Ensuring that children experience a positive emotional environment is key to their capacity and readiness to enter into effective learning.

 Key Point

- Make regular audits of provision areas to ensure that they motivate and engage children in challenging, problem-solving experiences.

Reflective Activity

How do you ensure that you have provided a variety of resources that are inviting and interesting, and can be used in open-ended ways to challenge children's thought and understanding? List 6 resources and, for each, record different ways that these could be used to challenge children's learning.

An inclusive environment

The current inclusion agenda uses the term 'vulnerable', as it reflects upon a varied list of children who display a range of differing needs. When thinking about inclusion, it is of key importance that practitioners have a 'can do' ethos in offering inclusive opportunities for learning. Practitioners need to share ideas and support other members of the team in overcoming the possible barriers to inclusion, by designing practical solutions for organisation and curriculum delivery.

One important question you should ask is, 'Does my planning, resource purchasing and classroom organisation reflect a commitment to inclusive practice?' If the answer to any part of this is 'no', it is probably time to rethink the way you are interpreting and addressing inclusion. It is not enough to show that you are aware of the term 'inclusion' without having the observable practice in place to fully support it.

There are a range of simple guidelines that need to be considered as a way of building in inclusive practice. From the earliest point of contact with parents and new admissions, does the literature and documentation you share with them welcome differing needs and offer examples of how such needs are supported? Do you accommodate flexible admission procedures and have books, posters and other resources that reflect differing cultures, social groups and children with different needs?

The environment should be inclusive of all children regardless of gender or race, and those with additional needs must be equally considered to enable the necessary support to be put into place. Once again their needs may influence the planning of the environment and the possibility of developing and changing areas.

 Case Study: Nursery: Catherine, aged 3 years and 6 months

The following case study gives a clear example of the issues and organisational decisions that had to be made to facilitate an effective and safe learning environment for one little girl with visual impairment.

As a teacher of a large nursery class, I was concerned at the forthcoming admission of Catherine, who was severely visually impaired with an assessment of needs that registered her as 85 per cent blind. Although the visually impaired services recommended a specialist support school, her parents were keen that she attend a mainstream school in their local area.

At the first meeting it was very apparent that Catherine was extremely independent, had a positive attitude to her own learning, and was eager to join other children in a social learning setting. The nursery team worked closely with the local authority support worker in understanding the logistics of presenting the kind of purposeful, safe and secure environment for this little girl. We wanted to ensure that Catherine continued to learn in a secure setting that would allow her to make her own choices for learning. In preparing for her safety, we remained equally aware of the needs of the other children and their right to equal opportunities for learning.

She was initially introduced to the layout of both the indoor and the outdoor environment to enable her to move confidently around the setting. We were advised that once she was more familiar with this, any future changes, such as introducing new areas of play provision that involved moving furniture, should be kept to a minimum. When we needed to reorganise, the new design was shared with her as early as possible, in order that she could readjust to the new structure. Brightly coloured tape was applied to the floor along the corridors of the school to guide her to the hall and dining areas, and she was always supported by a member of the team. The children were told about our new arrival prior to her admission. Like all children, Catherine had her own very unique needs and we were there to support and welcome her into our setting. Children were reminded of important health and safety considerations – for example, the fact that she may not see them as quickly as other children would. We shared useful strategies with them and reinforced that because Catherine may not always see them as quickly as other children might, they should stand in front of her to be in full vision in order to talk with her. We accessed training by the visually impaired services, and gained knowledge of the range of resources that were available to support children with visual learning difficulties, such as magnification monitors, and how to use them. By having Catherine as a member of our nursery, children acquired a heightened understanding of and sensitivity to individual difference. The team gained confidence and skills in providing effective support for children with visual difficulty, such as the use of large, brightly coloured resources and manipulative props, to ensure they have equal access to learning experiences.

1. Make a list of the concerns you may have if a child with similar learning needs was to be part of your setting.
2. Think about a child you have taught that had a particular learning need; how did you support them and how do you know your support was effective?

The emotional environment

The emotional environment is created by all the people in the setting, but adults have to ensure that it is warm and accepting to everyone (DCSF 2008a).

This concept can be strengthened by using the key person system, which is referred to in the EYFS. A key person has special responsibilities for working with a small number of children and their families. 'Key person' was the term that was first used to describe work that was taking place in nurseries in an attempt to provide children with a person to whom they could relate in a special way

(Goldschmeid and Jackson 2004). The key person's role is to ensure that the group of children for whom she or he is responsible are happy and feel safe. One of the essential duties of this role is to build positive relationships with parents and carers as a point of contact. The emotional well-being of children only occurs when they feel safe and secure; this means that their key person must be involved with them and their families, in order to know their needs, interests and their stage of development. Susan Isaacs was particularly interested in children's emotional development and recognised the impact poor treatment from adults could have on this. She believed it was essential that children's self-directed play and learning were prioritised with minimum interference from adults, whose role was mainly to observe children's learning in order to inform their future planning and identify their individual needs (cited in Daly et al. 2006).

Young children very quickly become aware and know whether adults like them and their families or not. The key person must obviously be aware of this and how this can impact on children's emotional development and consequently the child's learning. In order to develop the emotional environment, it must be a place where practitioners accommodate the needs of all children and adults. Children need to have opportunities to enter into a variety of activities, that allow them to experience a range of emotions in order to make sense of them. There need to be planned experiences, such as circle time, that allow children to say how they feel. By identifying their personal feelings and relationships with others supported by adults, children can then begin to learn important skills in handling their own emotions.

To support children and enable them to develop positive self-esteem, it is essential that

- They are with like-minded people – the children and adults they are with accept their interests.

- Children feel at home and relaxed and their learning is nurtured by adults who have developed a secure, safe, inclusive and challenging environment.

- The learning environment is a place where children and their family belong – it reflects the diversity of the community.

- They are able to respond in their own way and at their own level.

- The setting is a place where they feel secure and at ease – familiar routines and expectations.

A successful way of ensuring that children feel valued and their ideas are taken into consideration is to engage in a simple thought-shower activity to explore their ideas and interests. This is discussed in Chapter 5, where it is suggested that ideas can be easily recorded on a 'mind map', which can then inform future ideas for planning. Figure 3.2 was collated as a result of a conversation with a child who had recently visited 'Butterfly World' with his grandparents. He rushed into the setting and was eager to tell everyone about the magic butterflies he had seen with his grandma and grandad that weekend that could change all on their own from little, yellow caterpillars into beautiful, blue butterflies. He happily shared his experiences with the other children, who were able to contribute their own unique ideas and join in his awe and wonder moment. His enthusiasm was something that we had to capture, and we encouraged all the children to share their thoughts and current knowledge about butterflies and record them on a simple mind map. At the next planning meeting, staff made decisions as to the kind of experiences we could provide that would build not only his learning but would also offer meaningful experiences for all the children. These ideas would inform both continuous areas of provision and any future adult-led learning based upon our theme, 'Butterflies'.

According to the DCSF, 'when children feel confident in their environment they are willing to try things out, knowing their efforts are valued' (DCSF 2008c: 3.3).

Ways of learning

Effective early years learning environments need an appropriate balance of adult-led and child-initiated opportunities for learning. The EPPE report (Sylva et al. 2004) suggests a crucial balance of child-initiated versus adult-led learning is essential to offer positive learning experiences in the early years. When researching effective provision for the early years, they looked at what needed to happen as part of high-quality experiences for children. The study defined the balance as a 3:2 ratio in favour of child-initiated opportunities, and not a

Water Play

Using colours to mix with oils
Separating colours – jelly play
Gloop
Introducing coloured plastic paper
Mixing colours
Printing from surface oils

Book/Quiet Area

Books relating to butterflies: The
  Hungry Caterpillar
The Big Beautiful Butterfly
Dora the Explorer
Story sacks/puppets, plastic food,
  resources re-telling story

Numeracy Problem Solving Area

Sequencing days of the week
Time; clocks
Timing activities, sand clocks, ICT
  whiteboard digital timer
Counting patterns
Patterning sequences

Literacy/Mark-Making Area

Creative writing activities; the life cycle of a
  butterfly
Writing patterns in roller balls, felt pens,
  paint pads
Sequencing events of a story
Introduce new vocabulary linked to topic;
  chrysallis, cocoon, egg, wings, change

Topic theme: Butterflies

ICT Exploratory Area

Observing butterflies in other countries
Jigsaw butterflies, life cycles
Food from around the world
Materials and food that take changes in their
  form: custard, jelly, ice

Creative Area

Symmetrical pattern making
Dance experiences – coloured scarves to
  reflect wings
Dance to represent life cycle of butterfly
Stained glass images
Tie dyeing activities
Butterfly mobiles
Still life drawings; sequences of life cycle

Sand Play

Finding butterflies, caterpillars, eggs, etc., in
  sand
Drawing patterns in sand
Writing patterns

Outdoor Activity and Visits

Day visit to Manor Heath to see butterflies
Playing with butterfly nets
Insect search
Hanging mobiles
Caterpillar hunt

Investigative Area

Magnifying glasses
Bug pots
Observation of outdoor collections
Insect lore, caterpillar world
Taking care of butterflies, feeding eggs

Figure 3.2   Butterflies planning, continuous provision and adult-led learning

50/50 balance of adult-led and child-led activity, as is often incorrectly communicated by practitioners in early years. What needs to be highlighted here is that quite a different way of defining the term 'child-initiated' emerges from a more primary school-based origin. In this definition, the term refers to 'small windows of choice' for children in what is generally a more formal environment, and is in fact an attempt to create a more playful element in the primary curriculum. This model describes a definition of child-initiated learning that comes with a great deal of adult input, as they usually determine specific content such as when the opportunities arise. Child-initiated time in school settings is sometimes interpreted as 'Golden Time', which is often a popular practice timetabled on Friday afternoon as an end-of-week event and used as a reward strategy, rather than an opportunity for self-chosen learning. In this period it is adults who largely determine what resources children may access, and their choices and rules will often limit how far the learning can be taken.

In early years settings, the true sense of 'child-initiated learning' is ongoing, carefully presented through continuous provision areas. These are freely accessed by all children in the setting and regularly evaluated by practitioners in order to assess their effectiveness and impact upon children's learning. It presents opportunities for independent and group-led learning, encouraging children to practise skills and inviting adults as co-players in their creative ideas for play.

Adults achieve this by ensuring that children's interests are met, and they are encouraged to have independence for personal choices in their learning. For children to consolidate learning and skills, it is important that they be allowed to revisit experiences and become fully engaged in what they do, over sufficient periods of time with minimal interruption. Bruner's concept of the spiral curriculum suggests that children's learning is of a higher quality when they are given opportunity to revisit previous activities, enabling them to consolidate their current understanding and extend their ideas. This perspective of learning can also be applied to play, where children are offered meaningful learning experiences through regular access to continuous provision areas carefully resourced by knowledgeable adults. Children make personal choices for their play and are able then to repeat and practise their skills and consolidate what they have learned.

Case Study: Nursery class, snack time

Read the following case study and think about how you might organise snack time to develop children's independence and maximise their opportunity for learning.

Several years ago I was lucky to participate in the Effective Early Learning (EEL) programme. One of the tasks was to monitor the areas and routines of the classroom, by making observations of the children using them at that time. The children's level of engagement in the areas was to be scored against the Leuven Scale of Involvement (Laevers 1994).

From looking at my observations it became obvious that at snack time (which the whole class had together), there was little engagement on the children's part, while the nursery staff, in contrast, were busy making sure that each child had the appropriate food and a drink. At the next nursery staff meeting, this was discussed and a plan of action designed that might encourage children to be more involved. Over the next week we implemented our plan to introduce continuous snack time by developing a snack area. We displayed images of food, had a designated snack table, gave the children a choice of food and drink, and encouraged the children to use their registration cards to indicate if they liked the snack or not. When I returned to my observations, I found that the level of involvement had increased for all children and there was evidence of far greater independence.

1. Can you think of other strategies that could make snack time a more meaningful learning experience for children?
2. What benefits, if any, do you think there are of organising whole-class snack time?

🔑 Key Point

- Make sure that children have time to investigate, return to and repeat activities and experiences, to build upon what they know and have already learnt.

In the EYFS practice guidance (DCSF 2008b: 7), child-initiated learning is described as 'when a child engages in a "self-chosen pursuit"'. Children's focus for learning may be instigated, for example, when they bring something into the setting, such as an item from home that interests them, or even share a personal experience they may have had, such as visiting a hospital. Effective practitioners can follow the child's lead here by engaging in meaningful conversation with them and providing suitable resources, perhaps creating a hospital role-play area in order to extend learning experiences. By using this approach, they are motivated by access to a meaningful learning environment, along with opportunity to engage in social interaction to promote particular avenues of exploration and discussion.

The adult role

The following explanation of the role of the practitioner in supporting children's learning can be applied to all practitioners working in early years settings and is taken from *The Foundation Stage Teacher in Action*, in which Margaret Edgington speaks of 'enabling children to learn' and describes the role clearly:

> Teachers enable each child to learn and develop by helping them to sustain their current interests, expand their knowledge and also by interesting them in new things. The role of the enabler involves her in using a number of teaching roles and strategies. ... Often she uses a combination of these strategies. Whichever approach she uses, she keeps the needs of the children in mind to help her determine the optimum moment for learning – the moment when the child wants to, or needs to learn. (Edgington 2004: 176)

Her opinions as to the role and essential skills of the practitioner assert the importance of suitably trained, highly qualified practitioners. In particular, she reinforces the concept of meeting children's needs in a personalised way. She considers that skilled practitioners use earlier assessment of children's learning to identify the most appropriate approaches for future teaching and learning experiences that build upon their interests.

Adults who work in early years environments need to have clarity about their own role, and feel valued and respected as part of an effective team. It is essential that information is shared among the team about individual children's specific needs, such as dietary and medical requirements and how these will be met. Of equal importance is the need to have a good understanding of current policies of the workplace and guidelines for expected practice, such as keeping records of personal involvement with particular children and making daily assessment. It is recommended that effective practice means seeking advice from other professionals who work closely with children and networking with those who have experience of supporting children with similar learning needs. In the case of children who have Special Educational Needs (SEN) or who have English as a second language (EAL), it is essential to be aware they will often develop skills at a different rate from those suggested in curriculum models. Such children can make huge progress in one area of development whilst little is recorded in another. This is particularly important learning and addresses the 'unique child' strand of the EYFS, which communicates the importance of planning activities and measuring learning that is matched to individual needs.

Key Point

- Make sure that children can make independent choices for learning, linked to their interests, needs and personal stage of development.

The adult not only sets up good-quality and stimulating areas of provision but must also value them by regularly adding to the areas, repairing and respecting the resources, and supporting children's learning as they engage within them. Your role as a practitioner needs to incorporate three key aspects of professional practice:

- Identifying children's needs.

- Assessing their individual stage of development.

- Intervening in play in order to support their current understanding and move their learning forward.

The timing and nature of interventions is very important, however, and you do need to plan for this. An important finding was identified in the EPPE report (Sylva et al. 2004). The report refers to the role of adults in early years settings and suggests that children's learning was best supported when practitioners came alongside them in their learning, were attentive, and responded to direct questions from children, adding their own extended comments. It is also suggested that the key purpose of practitioner-led experiences are that they offer children opportunity to enter into learning situations that are new to them and that they may not have discovered for themselves (Fisher 2004).

The key message here is to reinforce the way practitioners engage and relate to children and their ability to learn alongside them as active players in learning experiences. It is essential that practitioners demonstrate that they, too, are motivated and enthused and are able to challenge children's current understanding through carefully planned questioning that leads to further learning.

There are certain questions that you need to ask yourself. Do you encourage children to take the lead in their learning? How often are you following their actions and ideas? Are you planning in time for open-ended, child-initiated activities to allow adults to become involved in the play experience?

Children very quickly recognise when practitioners do not value their play and respond accordingly. It is important, then, that adults become involved and let children take the direction of play forward in their own way. It is clear that adults who make positive responses to children and are willing to join in their play contribute to children's levels of self-esteem and confidence. By engaging in child-led activity, adults are presented with first-hand opportunities to make accurate assessment of individuals' particular stage of learning and understanding.

Meade (Fisher 2004) suggests that it is during free play that children have the greatest opportunity to develop their mental abilities through hands-on experiences.

Research into brain development suggests that interactions and opportunity to enter into creative play experiences in the early years directly affect the way the brain is wired and encourage synaptic connections to form. It is these pathways of connective ideas that children recall and are then able to introduce into new learning experiences (Gmitrova and Gmitrov 2003).

Dunkin and Hanna suggest that it is by engaging with children and allowing their ideas to influence our reactions and shape our questioning that we make important impressions on their current levels of understanding and ability to learn:

> When we as educators engage in such interactions with children, we are facilitating their journey as they search for answers and make meaning in the world. (Dunkin and Hanna 2001: 44)

By engaging in meaningful discussion with children, practitioners are able to scaffold children's current understanding and take the learning into new and challenging directions.

Building on children's interests and using their own ideas for learning and play are a key part of effective practice. In Reggio Emilia, children's interests and ideas are an integral part of this curriculum approach to learning. These interests influence long-term projects that often extend opportunities for exploration and learning. Contributions from parents are encouraged and they, too, spend time in the setting enjoying experiences alongside their children. In a similar way Friedrich Froebel identified 'free flow' play as an essential way of learning for children in their early years. He suggested that it is when children are happily engaged in playful, self-chosen activity that they are able to experiment with resources and materials and develop an understanding of how things work (cited in Daly et al. 2006).

It is conclusive that to provide an enabling environment requires a range of key considerations for effective practice. It is important that we respond to children's interests in a positive way, offering them a secure environment in which to learn and engaging adults in the learning experiences. By looking at alternative and successful approaches to learning such as Reggio Emilia and High Scope, we can clearly observe many aspects of good practice, such as effective parent partnerships and following children's interests. Making effective assessment is clearly dependent upon the environment in which children learn, the challenges the environment presents, and the understanding and skills of suitably skilled and informed practitioners.

Further Reading

Bayley, R., Bilton, H., Broadbent, L. et al. (2008) *Like Bees, not Butterflies: Child-Initiated Learning in the Early Years*. London: A & C Black.

- Written by a group of authors with extensive experience in early years practice, offering personal examples to show the importance of child-initiated learning.

London Borough of Lewisham (2002) *A Place to Learn: Developing a Stimulating Environment*. London:s LEARN.

- Great ideas here for planning a quality environment, with a range of suggested layouts and organisation.

Useful Websites

www.cego.be/

- additional information on *Ferre Laevers*.

www.highscope.uk.org

- information on the ethos, practice and outcomes of the High Scope approach to learning.

www.everychildmatters.org.uk

- essential website to explore the rationale, practice and policy of the *Every Child Matters* agenda.

Personalised learning: looking at children holistically

Julie Percival

Chapter Objectives

- To briefly consider the individuality of children's development, set in the context of the social world through which children build their understanding.
- To assert the need for personalised provision for well-being: teaching and caring based on holistic, multi-layered assessment.
- To consider planning as a process that is designed from the start to be a 'window on children's thinking', helping adults and children to look for the learning.
- To consider key concepts that help us frame our looking.

Within recent policy initiatives for schools, personalised learning has a specific definition. It is envisaged that personalised learning involves teachers in

> taking a highly structured and responsive approach to each child's and young person's learning, in order that all are able to progress, achieve and participate. It means strengthening the link between learning and teaching by engaging pupils – and their parents – as partners in learning. (Gilbert in DCSF 2007: 5)

Within the Early Years Foundation Stage (EYFS) (DCSF 2008) documentation, the principle of responding to the child's individual needs is woven throughout the themes and commitments, the

Statutory Framework (DCSF 2008a), the Practice Guidance (DCSF 2008b), and Principles into Practice cards (DCSF 2008c). In your setting or placement, you are prompted by the framework to consider how you care for and provide for the learning of each unique child. Through reading and reflection, you are supported to consider how the positive relationships that you build through your daily interaction demonstrate the respect you have for each other (children, families and colleagues together). Support and partnership for each child and their family comes primarily through the key person, who should reassure them that the child is 'safe and cared for' (DCSF 2008c: Themes and Commitments card).

For all practitioners, be they in school or sessional/full days care settings, the challenge of meeting individual needs whilst supporting groups of children can be daunting. It is unrealistic to set a goal of capturing every aspect of learning arising from a particular activity for each individual. We can only 'fall short' if this is the aspiration underpinning our assessment procedures (Drummond 2003: 54).

Ages and stages and checklists

Robinson (2008) notes that the passage of time gives a child's development a 'trajectory' that implies linear progression in one direction – that we should be able to 'map out a path' for each child and, with well-structured targets, stay on course. However, we are not only physical beings with senses that trigger certain behaviours; we have emotional senses that lead us to feel and behave in certain ways. Experiences and the ways in which we organise them and feel about them 'mingle' with our physical development to 'shape' us. As we grow and change, 'nothing happens in isolation – it is the whole child at work' (Robinson 2008: 149). It is understandable to feel bewildered by the maze of interconnecting developments. Textbooks often devote chapters, if not books, to single domains of development and learning such as cognition, emotions, language, brain development (neuroscience) and physical development. These interconnecting domains of development, it is suggested, unfold to a timetable that is personal to each child, yet this development is influenced by the 'global' ages and stages that are set out by theorists and researchers as universal facts. Theory is useful, but it requires our active engagement rather than unquestioning acceptance. Personalised learning in the early years is about adults providing a framework of opportunities for children to learn how to learn. Checklists of development or curriculum content may be helpful from time to time, but you are in a partnership of discovery which should be carefully nurtured as a result of observations that have been shared. From shared understandings, adults and children together decide on next steps.

Connecting with a child's experience of the world

Transformative approaches to supporting children and families are wary of adopting universal theories to explain an individual's development. An ecological theory of human development (Bronfenbrenner 1979) that places the child at the centre of layers of environmental influences and interactions is a starting point for thinking about the many factors influencing what and how children learn. The EYFS acknowledges the impact that the family and setting have on each child's development. The wider community is similarly acknowledged. As with the developmental, constructivist approach, children are seen as active participants in their learning. However, in this framework for thinking, the wider structures within society also contribute to this growing understanding through the interplay of a whole range of discourses and national policy initiatives.

> ### ⚷ Key Points
>
> - Learn about the children and the aspects of their life that help make them who they are. In dialogue with children, their families and colleagues, you may consider their faith, the social customs of their family and their particular use of language.
> - Use your ever-changing knowledge of the child to inform your curriculum *and* the assessment process.
> - Think about thinking! Children build their thinking around their social world. When you plan for investigating, creating and problem solving, set your activities in familiar contexts so children are not struggling to make sense of new situations, and they can focus on the learning.
> - Help the child to be an 'apprentice' (Rogoff 1999). An apprentice actively contributes to the workplace from the start. How are
>
> *(Continued)*

children given space to be active agents who contribute to the life of the setting? How are their contributions valued?

- Learn about the systems and routines in your setting, the language staff use, and the activities and resources chosen. Then ask questions. Here are just a few:

  o Who makes the decisions? Why?
  o Who does more of a particular activity and why?
  o Who takes up practitioner time and why?
  o What takes up practitioner time and why?

Do all children have a fair and just opportunity to be who they are and to learn in and through ways that respect their lives outside the setting?

The term 'assessment' seems to imply something precise and measurable, and yet, as indicated thus far, children's development and learning are complex, deeply embedded in their emotional well-being, their own personal dispositions in organising interpretations of their experiences, their biological make-up, and the social world in and through which they live. How can practitioners working in the context of a busy classroom or group care setting assess children to support personalised learning or individualised provision for care, development and learning?

Personalised learning requires personalised care

In the EYFS, we start by getting to know a person – a new member of our community – and making space for them to be the unique person that they are. Resting, playing, sleeping, eating, drinking, getting dirty, becoming clean, going to the toilet, feeling well and sometimes not, needing space and needing to be close to the right person, doing nothing then being deeply engrossed (do not disturb!), having a choice, being cherished – all these fundamental behaviours, needs or feelings and more happen at home, in a familiar place where most feel secure and loved. For substantial periods of the day, some babies and young children are cared for outside their home. For some, they will be with a childminder (and possibly an assistant) in their home; for others, they will be one of many children living out their personal, intimate lives in an establishment that may or may not look or feel anything like their home. Day care is not necessarily about reproducing home or the intimate, close relationships between those who live there (Dahlberg and Moss in Elfer et al. 2003), but we can appreciate some of what a child may be feeling when we reflect on how comforting it is to return to our own space when we have been visiting even the closest of friends.

Effective early years practitioners who work in care-based settings must be tuned into the fundamentals of life. Their observations of children and their reflections on those observations must include assessments of children's need for and response to such things as solid foods and their preference for going to sleep after lunch with their particular blanket and a particular soothing tune. Personalised provision that considers children as individuals is absolutely vital for each unique child within your group. When the fundamentals of life are addressed through imposed routines delivered by an unresponsive hand, institutionalised practice becomes embedded. Acceptance sets in. Practitioners may feel overwhelmed by the numbers of dinners to get through or the nappies to be changed. The routine task becomes more important than the feelings and specific needs of all concerned. When we as adults face the 'one size fits all' approach to being cared for, it disturbs us. We can rationalise the reasons why we might have been treated in such a way. Children need you to observe sensitively and use what you have learned about them to decide how you will care for them and support their learning. Damaging institutionalised care is not inevitable. The following case study shows how one student was able to compare the practice of two very different settings.

 Case Study: Reflections on two placement experiences

As you read about one student's observations of provision for groups of children, consider how important care is to ensuring personalised learning is possible.

A student on placement was working alongside an experienced practitioner and a group of 2- and 3-year-olds as they made chocolate cereal buns. As equipment and ingredients needed to be passed around the table and wriggling bodies got on and off

(Continued)

chairs, it became clear that the children did not know each other's names. 'That girl … she's got all the chocolate!', one person exclaimed. 'You need to sit down!', the practitioner said, leaning over to stop the contents of a box of cereal being eaten by the handful. This set the student thinking about her previous placement and how Sam (aged 3) always seemed to know when it was time to eat …

It's lunchtime. Sam knows it because the cook has come through the door. He's really hungry and has been checking the signals that it's getting time to eat. The whole room smells good too! Together the cook and Sam wipe the tables and others join in to lay out the cutlery. He has his own damp cloth and rubs the table vigorously. 'Looking good, Sam!', the cook comments. Around the room, as games come to an end, they are put away. Babies are 'checked' to make sure they are comfortable. A toddler has a quick visit to the potty. The big book chest is dragged out and children place their carpet square round the box in readiness. The huge lid is opened. A practitioner and two children are still engrossed in reading but they are nearly finished as around them everyone else, children and adults alike, share in the 'getting ready'. Soon, the small nursery is brought together. No one has said stop: all have been purposefully engaged in getting ready for lunch. The rhymes and props and pictures from a big book are the focus of everyone's attention, from the babies sitting with their key person to the older children wriggling, jiggling, singing, sign-ing, listening and looking. Every adult is participating, singing with and to the children near them.

Each person, in their own way, has contributed to this coming together. Each takes pleasure in the words and sound, actions and gestures. The meal trolley comes out. Some are hands washed and at the table in an instant, but others linger over the big book of rhymes or enjoy a 'Round and round the garden' tickle one more time. There is laughter and discussion as all select from the range of food available and eat together.

The student on placement is brought back to the baking activity – someone is tugging the baking bowl and someone else wants to leave the table.

Personalised provision is possible but it is multi-layered. Adopting a blueprint from a textbook will not work, but asking questions about practice can most certainly help. The student in the case study had seen the web of personalised provision within the context of group care in action in one setting.

- Can you identify what it was that the practitioners chose to do to ensure that even during routines such as getting ready for lunch, there was opportunity for individual care and learning?
- How did the baking experience 'close down' the opportunities for personalised care and learning, even through each child had their own turn to do something?

The 'ethic of care' at work in a school

Using the Effective Early Learning process (Pascal and Bertram 1997), the reception and nursery class teams developed their underpinning 'ethic of care' (Dahlberg and Moss 2005: 91) to support more formal, classroom-based learning.

Systematically gathered observations led them to feel troubled by the way children returned to class after lunch: they decided to learn more about mealtimes, eventually deciding that this 'non–teaching' part of the day should be a main area for development, as it seemed to be having such an impact the children's day. The mealtime routine was renegotiated with lunchtime staff and parents. However, addressing well-being for the group had a tremendous impact on the emotional tone of the day, the amount each child ate, and the way they played during the lunch break as well as the 'involvement levels' in their learning (Laevers 1996, cited in Pascal and Bertram 1997) back in the classroom. Assessment of children during the whole of the day through sensitively gathered observation, evaluation and action can support personalised provision for learning. Ensuring that there are opportunities for personalised learning in the EYFS requires a good understanding of the dynamics of care in your setting.

Children observe, imitate, rehearse and practise (Robinson 2008) when someone in their day respectfully looks, listens and notes their behaviour, reads the signals, and uses the knowledge gained to fine-tune provision for holistic development and learning. But this is not about surveillance: it is about a pedagogy of listening (Dahlberg and Moss 2005; Rinaldi 2006). You observe but then you

- Try to hear the thinking and the feelings – what does the child's behaviour tell you?

- Ask open questions – your interpretation of events may not be the same as the child's.

Habits of mind are built on reciprocal relationships (Carr 2003). When you work in a way that does not presume you know all the answers, you can think about how you, the children, and their family can learn together. Children learn your habit of mind: the way you have learned to routinely think about them.

 Reflective Activity

Consider the following key messages.

- The way children feel about themselves is not innate or inherited, it is learned. (Siraj–Blatchford and Clarke 2000: 23)

- How babies and young children learn to see themselves is significantly affected by their growing knowledge of how to be acceptable to us. (Roberts 2002: 145)

Good-quality early years care does not happen by accident. What do babies and children learn from your routines, the way you touch them, your non-verbal communication, the way you speak and what you say, the resources you choose to set out for them, and the way you tackle your learning? What do you want them to learn from you? How will you know about the way they feel about themselves?

Why is assessment of this aspect of practice so vital?

Assessment for well-being enables practitioners to:

- Select particular teaching strategies to meet particular learning needs.

- Select particular approaches to care to meet particular developmental needs.

Personalised provision for learning and development is based on documenting experiences that form the basis discussion and analysis, enabling the selection of beneficial teaching and caring techniques for each child across the EYFS.

Towards a pedagogy of personalised learning

Guidance for school lists 9 features of personalised learning:

1. High-quality teaching and learning.

2. Target setting and tracking.

3. Focused assessment.

4. Intervention.

5. Pupil grouping.

6. The learning environment.

7. Curriculum organisation.

8. The extended curriculum.

9. Supporting children's wider needs.

As a framework for evaluating existing practice, it is of considerable use for school-based settings. However, the EYFS supports practitioners who work across 5 years of a child's life, only one of which could be a compulsory school year, depending on when the child is 5 years old. The 'major task' of learning to be a pupil and all that that entails (Kelly 1992: 41) can be more significant to a child of 4 or 5 than being aware of learning outcomes and achievement against those outcomes – especially if they were chosen and designed by someone else and the logic behind them is not clear from the child's perspective! It is therefore important to think carefully what these key features look like in the early years.

Planning for personalised learning and the role of assessment

In *Researching Effective Pedagogy in the Early Years*, Siraj-Blatchford et al. (2002) note the importance of knowledgeable adults carefully matching the curriculum to challenge children's thinking and so enhance cognitive progress. Planning for this to happen in a setting where a child is one of a group being supported by significantly fewer adults is quite a skill. It takes time and constant reflection because, not surprisingly, there are no set formulas that can be applied to the variety of settings working within the EYFS.

Planning for individual children does *not* mean that a series of one-to-one activities needs to be resourced, carried out and evaluated. The learning outcomes for each child are assessed and lead you to compile a personalised record. As a key person and/or teacher, you become aware of the individual's pattern of interests and learning styles, bank of emerging skills and knowledge, and independent abilities. This awareness develops clarity of focus when observations and notes of conversations are discussed and documented. These individual records inform the strategies you select for caring and teaching. 'On the job' differentiation complements more formal plans, which are made on the basis of discussions between

- Colleagues who have shared experiences with the child and observed them in the setting going about their learning.

- Parents and children as they go about their lives together, experiencing the world and making sense of things together.

- Parents and the key person and/or teacher sharing their perspectives on the child's learning and development.

- The child and the key person and/or teacher as they build their history of experiences together.

Planning is your aide memoire – not a straitjacket

(As you read the following sections, you will see that the key features of personalised learning in the early years are printed in italics.)

In the short term planning captures the ideas you have about *what* children might need to learn and *why*. It reminds you *how* an activity or concept could be introduced and the different ways in which resources and spaces could be used. Well-designed planning also signposts what you will be interested in finding out and assessing.

There will be talk as new words are explored, questions are posed and commentary given. Your *talk will vary* according to the needs of the child. Sometimes *silence* will be required and your plan will remind you when to step back and remain quiet. Your plan will also prompt you to bring children together in *different groupings* depending on their needs or interests and you will have thought carefully about the contribution different people will bring to the learning.

You will avoid narrow planning that is based on tasks that lead to a disheartening and narrow range of behaviour for adults to observe and children to reflect on. Some practitioners may resort to creating test-like assessment tasks to check up and facilitate formal recording of a certain type of learning for accountability purposes. Sometimes these tasks masquerade as play! Your planning will avoid this too!

Ongoing formative assessment

Throughout the implementation of the plan, you will be observing children's actions in an attempt to *understand their thinking*. This ongoing assessment of the child's thought processes and the child's meaning-making, as the learning is taking place, helps you to decide how to offer support to sustain their interest. Your evaluation of the plan will note *significant developments* (Hutchin 2000) in each child's thinking, new understandings they have demonstrated, or new skills they have used. When understanding and skills have been applied in a different context, this generalised learning will also be noted.

Supporting the learning

In supporting the child's learning, you avoid too many questions. Your *commentary* during the activity supports children in thinking about their learning and the context in which it is being learned. The *feedback* you gave as the activity takes place also supports the children in *thinking about the learning*. You make it specific so that positive comments are linked to observable behaviour. You are aware that positive comments and constructive support when problems arise help children to see their own problem solving as effective, with tasks being achievable given time, creative thinking and persistence. You *consider* how praise can contribute to children being passive learners if the social reward becomes more meaningful than the sheer pleasure (or frustration!) of making new connections and judging for themselves what the meaning and consequences of new experiences are (Brooker 2008).

Reflect and interpret

When *you and the children reflect* on the session (or their day), you discuss how the experience went. In the 'high-scope' approach, some children will be able to set daily plans for themselves. They will review them at the end of each session, using *props to prompt reflection* such as pieces of equipment from areas of continuous provision, children's work, photographs and short video footage of events during the day. This seemingly anecdotal approach to looking back is supported through careful talk that focuses on 'language for thinking,' creativity, reasoning, investigation and problem solving. Summative judgements and comparison of individual performances are rare in these discussions.

Dialogue including open questions helps the practitioner to identify and develop each child's ability to assess for themselves and prioritise their possible next steps. Perhaps it is more appropriate to move away from the word 'assessment' and suggest that this process is akin to narration: through the storytelling (in all its many forms) comes relistening, reseeing, revisiting and 'recognition' of *interpretations of learning* (Rinaldi 2006: 58).

Planning for the next session on the basis of daily reviews

For the very youngest children, practitioners will take the last part of their working day as a short, team-planning session. This essential review of informal and formal observations is the basis for the fine tuning of provision to meet individual needs ready for the next day (Post and Hohmann 2000) and often includes conversations with parents and carers. Personalised learning relies on both this informal and formal assessment.

And so you and your team reflect on your activities. You consider events that have taken place as the children have interacted with the freely chosen continuous provision. What has been significant about the day? New plans might be made, old plans might be revised, continuous provision may be adapted – all the while you keep to the fore *why* you are making the decisions and plans you do: you are looking for a *window on children's thinking* so that you can best meet their intellectual, emotional and physical needs. Drawing on transformational principles, you consider the dynamics of the community that is your setting.

How do children collaborate? How are resources such as adult time, equipment and space being shared so that learning is maximised and just for all? How are children being supported to appreciate how they learn from and contribute to the social capital that is their setting? Personalised learning in the early years lays the foundations for each and every child to appreciate their own agency and the positive and unique contribution they can make to the agency of others.

Medium-term planning

Coherence and equity come through the medium-term plan. This is an opportunity to look more broadly at what will possibly be on offer for the next few weeks. Fundamentally, all in the team should be involved in this overview because patterns in the learning across the setting will inform choices made about how routines for care will run, how assessments will be planned for, the key concepts and patterns of thinking that will be nurtured, and the focus of any additional adult intervention. After reviewing the learning diet thus far, the team may decide that particular interests can be extended through exciting new opportunities such as visits of visitors. Trends in the patterns of relationships and structures within the group emerge, and it is this looking back and interrogation with an open mind that preserves equity. Do systems and routines support each child to make a positive contribution (DfES 2004)? It is too late to review the way the principles are being played out at the end of the year. The dynamics of the group can have a powerful impact on the personal learning of each child. Using the short-term planning cycle alone limits the assessment opportunities for both practitioner and child.

Long-term planning

In the long term, teams review the balance and breadth of their offer to children and families. They plan for the next year by having a clear rationale for the continuous provision, the selection of themes to sustain children's passions and open up their horizons, and the overall systems for allocating resources and space. The richness of this provision and the practitioner's awareness of its potential for teaching and learning ensure that over the year, there is flexibility to meet the needs of individual children. In a sense, the ingredients are all available and prepared so that the variety of meals that can be created by both children and adults is infinite.

Key concepts in early years assessment for personalised learning

Observing children's thinking and self-assessments (schema)

Careful observation will reveal how self-assessment is part of the child's daily life. Personalised provision requires practitioners to interpret these particular assessments and the context in which they occur, and the impact they have on learning should also influence the plans you make. Children who see themselves as capable, independent learners will automatically make judgements about the quality of their actions. They will persist and solve problems until they have reached their satisfactory conclusion.

For Athey (2007), our understanding of children's mental actions can only be 'construed' from representations 'such as symbolic play, drawing, brick constructions and the like' (Athey 2007: 55). These representations of thought or schema appear as repeatable patterns of behaviour, like working hypotheses that children use for making sense of the world. Schema can be observed and analysed. The process of learning is more important than the store of facts or the acquisition of a particular skill. For a child, their patterns of behaviour are strategies for learning. They self-assess the impact of their actions on the environment and choose further behaviour in the light of the schema or schemas that they have found useful in the past. Sensitive adults nurture a child's inbuilt desire to learn. They plan their own interventions based on careful analysis, understanding that children have opinions about their actions too.

There are a considerable range of schemas or working theories that children use to help them make sense of the world and their experiences. Working with this theoretical concept enables adults to appreciate that children can meet new situations without worrying about lack of knowledge. They can be seen as experimenters, able to make judgements in action, constantly searching for personal meaning. Once they become aware of the (social) significance of the 'right' way to do things (and the converse), they become constrained by the need to perform within a subject-based curriculum. Within the EYFS, personalised learning can be planned for effectively if adults are able to tune into the 'within child' cognitive structures that support early learning. The well-resourced, rich, continuous provision available in many early years settings allows children to plan their own learning content, with their own developing range of cognitive structures (schemas) supporting the process of learning.

Dispositions

A key element of personalised provision lies in adult's ability to assess children's propensity to utilise their growing knowledge and skills.

For Carr (2001), the decisions and choices adults make should be informed by the child's 'situated learning outcomes', not by a subject-based curriculum. The EYFS framework (DCSF 2008a) requires that progress in the six areas of learning must be tracked. The aspect dispositions and attitudes can be found within personal, social and emotional development (PSED), but it would be useful to examine Carr's layers of dispositional behaviour.

1. They acquire skills and knowledge – for them to be useful, children needs to be *aware that they possess them and can use them at will*, thus

2. Skills and knowledge + intent = learning strategies that they can apply when using the tools of life or working and playing with others.

3. Learning strategies + social partners, practices + tools = situated learning strategies that can be called upon in appropriate contexts.

4. Situated learning strategies + motivation = disposition to learn.

Carr further defines the levels of disposition that children may exhibit in their play and general behaviour. The thrill of working with a child (or colleague!) that is ready, willing and able to tackle anything means you will never be bored working in early years! Possible lines of development are at their richest when they build on observed schema and careful analysis of what is the most likely context for nurturing dispositions. For all learners, the relationship with the teacher (be that a parent, a practitioner or a peer) must be founded on reciprocity and responsiveness. The trust that such relationships engender means that children can give themselves up to an activity without fear of negative consequences. Children with a strong disposition to learn lack self-consciousness and find intrinsic reward in their activity; they can see a clear goal and have a sense of purpose.

Co-constructing the learning

Siraj-Blatchford et al. (2002) suggest that effective practitioners offer an instructional element in their interactions with children, perhaps by describing relevant facts or demonstrating ways of tackling tasks that scaffold the learning but do not take control away from the child. However, carefully chosen, open-ended questions and the role modelling of particular techniques and processes are also advocated. Their research indicated that increased cognitive outcomes for young children are associated with the joint involvement of both parties, especially when sustained over time and through the mutual interest and challenge. It is significant that both bring knowledge or skill to the activity; however, 'a good grasp of the appropriate pedagogical content knowledge' is also seen as a 'vital component' (Siraj-Blatchford et al. 2002: 11) in most cases. The adult (but possibly another child with useful appropriate knowledge) decides when to introduce new information on the basis of ongoing in-action formative assessment and previous judgements about the child's learning needs.

Through reflection in action and, later, reflection on action (Schon 1987), the practitioner actively interprets and assesses a child's thinking and formulates theories to enable the further scaffolding of the child's learning. This highly personalised provision for learning through sustained shared thinking (Siraj-Blatchford et al. 2002) is possible in the context of small-group work but also arises naturally in some play contexts. A rich environment for play is a vital source of child-initiated, sustained, shared thinking opportunities that watchful, sensitive adults can pick up on. Every adult who works with young children knows the value of time spent in unhurried exploration and the reciprocity of mutual regard. Nothing informs assessment like knowing how to be together, where challenge is not threatening (or driven by targets) but exciting and rewarding (and driven by motivation and a sense of creative thinking).

Play

Definitions of play are numerous and the case for a play-based curriculum does not need to be made here. Provision for play that is richly resourced and informed by ideas as to how children learn, and their interests and dispositional development is fundamental to personalised learning in the early years. Play may be children's work, but perhaps the divide between play and work should not be made.

Play does not become 'legitimate' because we liken it to work. Play is a serious endeavour and integral to the planning and assessment cycle. It is a way of making universal provision, within which individual children can control their own learning and adults can scaffold new learning. Children can learn from each other without too much fear of failure. Watchful adults will ensure that each child's entitlement to play is protected. Play should be resourced with the rich variety of cultural artefacts available to children, but should also be supplemented by collections of the unusual and the natural, sometimes linked by themes, supporting emerging interests and extending established interests.

Target setting and tracking

> Precise target setting and rigorous and regular tracking of progress towards these targets can be seen as underpinning personalised learning. (DCSF 2008a: 14)

Keeping children 'on trajectory', as advocated by the personalised learning guidance, implies that we know and can control children's learning as if they were units of production. At a time when we may be pushed further into ticking boxes and putting numbers against children, it is important to see the rigour in what is advocated by those who have researched and developed sound early years practice. It is important to resist precise targets that narrow children's opportunities to be connected to their passions, their culture and real-world experiences (Marsh 2005). Personalised learning in the early years is underpinned by discussion and decision making, which in turn are based on documentary evidence that has been thoughtfully collated by children and adults together.

The richness and authenticity comes from capturing the unique responses children make, and the variety of ways they represent their understanding and demonstrate their ability to apply concepts and skills. Learning stories (Carr 2003) and learning journey documents capture learning over time and show progress. They are all the more pertinent when children and their parents and carers have had some responsibility in gathering evidence, and reviewing and evaluating progress.

Evaluations and commentaries need to be linked to the EYFS, as this is the current framework for practice. Many local authorities and settings are working together to ensure that there are systems in place to enable practitioners to track individual progress over time, using the learning and development grids. Goldstein (2008) is pragmatic and argues that it is possible to complete a certain amount of formal record keeping that summarises outcomes, whilst considering the processes and the richness of children's learning. This type of record keeping should not dominate your practice but does serve an important function. You need to challenge the data generated by these whole-group tracking methods so that you can be sure that *all* children are being cared for in ways that respect who they are. You may even need to consider if the information that feeds into the tracking sheets has been arrived at in ways that give an authentic picture of children's learning and development. Above all, the information from tracking sheets must prompt you to identify any barriers to care and learning and do something about them!

⊶ Key Points

Personalised learning can take many forms: almost any planning format will work if opportunities, activities and routines are carefully chosen and based on a clear rationale and flexible strategies for teaching and care. Fundamentally, you and the children are learning how to learn – something we do from birth! Aim to:

- Learn what children can do, their passions and their personal history – this starts with respectful dialogue with families and children.
- Learn when, how and why to offer your support – it will be different for different children.
- Have materials readily available so that you can respond to a spontaneous need to explore, create or solve a problem when it needs doing.
- Learn to adapt resources or activities in response to a child's approach to learning.
- Liaise with other professionals or use a toy library to ensure specialist equipment is available as needed.
- Secure bilingual support as needed – but learn some new words and phrases yourself.
- Use the environment creatively, because you know that learning can be a physical, active, messy and sometimes boisterous business.

And document and celebrate the learning together – children, families and practitioners!

Personalised learning is possible when the interaction between practitioner and child 'fits'. The 'fit' between what children need for their learning and what adults offer through their teaching and care is more likely to be successful if assessment for learning (and for accountability) captures how children learn as well as what they learn.

Further Reading

Dahlberg, G. and Moss, P. (2005) *Ethics and Politics in Early Childhood Education.* London: RoutledgeFalmer

- A complex but useful discussion that places the 'ethic of care' at the centre of pre-school practice.

Useful Websites

www.teachernet.gov.uk/publications [accessed May 2009].

- DCSF (2008) *Personalised Learning: A Practical Guide.* London: DCSF. This is a document produced to support practice in schools. It is interesting to compare this with guidance from the CD-ROM (and online resources) that forms part of the EYFS (DCSF 2008).

To see how this initiative fits in with the *Every Child Matters* agenda, you could go to **www.everychildmatters.gov.uk/ete/personalisedlearning/** [accessed May 2009].

5

Listening to children and each other

Denise Chadwick and Anne Webster

Chapter Objectives

- To consider the purpose and importance of self and peer assessment in children's learning and development.
- To explore the range of creative strategies practitioners use when supporting children to enter into assessment activities.

This chapter explores the importance of using children's ideas, conversations and explanations of their involvement in play as a way of making assessment of their learning. It considers their skill and personal ability to effectively communicate and share ideas that enable adults to measure their current stage of development. The chapter refers to a number of government initiatives and considers the findings of early years research in order to analyse the rationale and success for making this kind of assessment and the useful strategies practitioners employ.

Mary Jane Drummond believed assessment is about seeing children's learning, understanding it, and then putting our understanding to good use (Drummond 1993). In order to do this, we need to keep the most important people in the whole process at the forefront of our mind and that is the children themselves. How much attention and time do we take to actually listen to what children are telling us about their learning and are their ideas considered in our assessment process? As skilled practitioners, we need to draw upon our knowledge of child development and theory and be ready to reflect upon the different ways that children learn. Most importantly, it is only when we have a broad range of evidence and information about each child that we can truly apply our understanding of theory to practice. So how can we use the different forms of assessment to meet children's personalised needs and support them effectively through their next stages of development?

An assumption that was described by Harry Torrance and John Pryor (1998) and termed 'convergent' assessment was that assessment sums up the child's knowledge or skill from a predetermined list. A more familiar term that practitioner's use is 'summative assessment', which provides a snapshot of attainment in one given moment and in preselected areas. Summative assessment is reflected in many pre-scribed tests used in educational practice today. It takes the form of tick lists of skills which are regularly updated or written tests admin-istered at the end of each school year, to sum up learning. In the early years an initial form of summative assessment was com-monly known as baseline assessment, and happened at point of entry to settings. This presented practitioners with a checklist of skills and specific areas of development, by which to measure chil-dren's levels of achievement. Many practitioners designed their own baseline formats that predominantly measured children's personal and social skills. In many cases these were the first recorded infor-mation about children's development, other than health records, to inform future planning. Some local authorities are now requiring practitioners to baseline children's attainment against the Early Years Foundation Stage Profile (EYFSP). At the end of the Foundation Stage, practitioners make a summative assessment of children's learning known as the EYFSP. This sums up and describes children's development and skills and measures their skills through six areas of learning against the early learning goals. It is important to recognise that all registered early years providers are legally required to complete individual profiles at the end of the academic year in which children reach the age of 5. These assessments are shared with parents and carers and recorded as e-profiles for local authority records.

It is important to remind the reader here about the importance of collecting evidence from parents and carers that will also contribute to the profile. Their contributions are essential if we are to present a holistic record of children's achievements and their preferred way of learning.

When we think about self-assessment and peer-assessment, it is more appropriate to consider an alternative form of assessment known as formative assessment, which emphasises the learner's understanding, and is jointly accomplished by the practitioner and the learner. A critical place for using assessment is at the start of the cycle of teaching and learning. Making assessment at this point, as well as at the end of a teaching experience, allows the practitioner to gain an accurate insight into children's current knowledge and a better understanding of how individuals prefer to learn. So how, then, do you actively set about gathering this information?

Firstly, you need to make observations of children in active learning situations, to slowly gather pieces of information about them, that will create a picture of what they can do and what they already know. I imagined this evidence as single pieces of an incomplete jigsaw that were gradually slotted together to make the whole image. Sometimes, inserting one piece could make a part of the jigsaw come to life, and what at first appeared little more than colour and pattern would suddenly change the whole representation and present a meaningful shape. In the same way, understanding what children are really all about, their likes and dislikes, skills and personalities, can be compared to a complex jigsaw, requiring many pieces of information to reach an accurate and meaningful assessment of each child. What is equally important is to have conversations with those people who know the child best, and hold key knowledge of them. To gather this broad base of information, you need to talk to a range of people, parents and carers, extended family members, siblings, peers and family friends.

This information you access will inform you about:

- What particularly interests the child; hobbies, people they like to spend time with, favourite television programmes and books.

- How the child perceives themselves as a learner; are they lacking in confidence in any particular aspect of new learning? Have they struggled to achieve new skills such as riding a bike or socialising with their peers?

- What the child can already do and what they have demonstrated that they know.

- What they are eager to know and do; join an activity club, or use a computer or interactive game.

By having conversations with people who know and spend time with the child, you will gain knowledge of them from different perspectives. This is really important, as those of us who have experience of working with children and may be lucky enough to have children of our own know only too well children's ability to demonstrate a range of behaviour that is dependent upon the context in which they find themselves. As a mother of two boys, I was reminded of this on numerous occasions when the younger of my sons would stay over at friend's house for an evening. On returning my thanks for their hospitality, I was regularly bombarded with responses that spoke about a son I could barely recognise, one who was so sociable and well mannered, offering to take out the rubbish and clear the dishes, and how they would willingly do a swap should I ever be interested. Who was this alien and why was it that, had I been asked to describe him, I would have offered a very different assessment of this very same child?

This scenario is very familiar and is often debated during informal conversation between parent and practitioner. Children display a range of behaviour according to the particular situation in which they find themselves, and because of this, they can appear very different to one observer as opposed to another. The implications here are that it is critical that conversations with parents and carers happen at the earliest point of contact in order to raise awareness of earlier assessment and so enable practitioners to have better understanding of children's personalities and traits.

We also need to understand what is really meant by effective assessment, assessment that is meaningful and accurate and offers us a holistic view of the individual. How do we access assessment that will enable us to support individuals to achieve in a way that they enjoy, engage with and learn best, and not just make assessment for assessment's sake?

We believe there are a set of determinants to consider, which are as follows:

- Have we considered the parents' and carers' contributions and their knowledge of the child throughout their educational experience?

- Are our assessments based on observations of the child in action, in situations of learning and exploration that are both self-initiated and adult-directed without predetermined outcomes?

- Are notes of significant development of skills and learning taken as they happen?

- Are we gathering assessment from a range of people who know the child best?

- Are we involving children, are they informed about what is written and are they given time to express their own opinion?

Listening to children

Talking to children about their learning provides an opportunity to personally reflect on their knowledge and understanding, and is helpful in getting to know the child well. Having a conversation with them helps us discover aspects of their current understanding that may otherwise have never been uncovered. However, making time to talk to children is an area of practice that is often missed, unless carefully and purposely planned. A possible reason for failing to use children's talk effectively as a tool for making assessment is due to the difficulty many children display in their earliest years in using language and conversation. Children's levels of speaking and listening and their skill in using language for communication have declined over the last decade. Research into understanding why this may be so suggests the growing influence of technology in all our lives. Television, email, and text messaging largely explain why many children fail to hear good models of language or have regular opportunity to enter into rich communication (Palmer 2007).

This worrying decline in the early development of good language skills in young children has informed educational policy for a number of years now. Government funding has been directed towards improving these 'low level' language skills through initiatives such as Talk to Learn, Chatter Matters, and the latest 'I Can' series of support initiatives. Teaching materials such as the Social and Emotional Aspects of Learning (SEAL) and more recent Social and Emotional Aspects of Development (SEAD), specifically designed for early years, have been introduced to schools and early years settings, to support children's personal, social and emotional development (PSED) and lead them to engage in purposeful talk with skilled practitioners.

Talking and learning together

Using effective communication with children as an assessment tool could be viewed as a point of reference for initial teacher training and continual professional development. Modelling how to use open-ended questioning to receive more than yes/no answers and generate confidence in talking with children is essential training, if we are to enter into meaningful dialogue with them. Dillon (Fisher 2004) claims that excessive questioning makes children dependent and passive. Alexander et al. (Fisher 2004) called for higher-order questioning to develop cognitive skills. This level of questioning to promote sustained, shared thinking also features as effective practice in learning and development, in the EYFS principles into practice cards and in the REPEY research. When we talk to children, are we really listening to what they tell us, or are we only looking for a pre-determined set of outcomes? The following excerpt gives an example of how practitioners realise that sometimes children's understanding differs from our own. This is a conversation that occurred between a nursery teacher and Hassan, a 5-year-old boy.

> Hassan was busy looking through his drawer. I asked him, 'What are you looking for, Hassan?' He replied, 'I'm looking for my diary.' 'What diary,' I asked? 'My diary,' he said. 'What does it look like?,' I asked. 'You know my diary!' At that moment Zain came along, looked at me, and said, 'He means his dictionary.'

This clearly shows how practitioners need to speak clearly, perhaps using objects to reinforce meaning, and check that children have a similar understanding of terminology to accurately interpret what has been said.

The richest forms of self-assessment come from situations where children enter into conversations with the adult, but it is they that do most of the talking. This often occurs when children are involved in self-initiated play and exploration, and the adult is happily included and involved in this play experience. Children's learning is often taken to a new level when an adult plays alongside them in a role-play area, for example, happily waiting to be seen by the doctor's receptionist or booking a holiday at the travel agent, modelling effective conversation, adding experiences of their own, and scaffolding play.

With children in early years it is important that we look for creative ways of making assessment of their learning. They, too, need to be introduced to the understanding and purpose of making assessment and why we are interested in hearing from them about what they like to do and what they have learnt.

The EYFSP states that 'Practitioners should fully involve children in their assessment by encouraging them to talk about and review their own learning' (DCSF 2008a: 9). To do this, we suggest you think about the following points:

- When playing alongside children, tell them what you are writing, share your findings with them, tell them what you thought was good. Invite them to add their own comments; this will encourage them to understand that you record positive comments about them and that they are being given opportunity to reflect and respond.

- For bilingual children and those with specific learning needs, you need to include visual support to help their understanding and allow them to contribute to the assessment.

- Remember to use facial expressions and gestures so that children can feel secure and tune in to your meanings.

- Share your records regularly with children to praise and consolidate their learning and have an opportunity to talk about what might be their next steps in learning.

It is important that children be involved at every stage in their own assessment and that they see assessment as a natural part of their learning process. As with any new skill, they need time to practise and explore, before they improve and finally master the skill. If a child does not respond the first few times you talk to them about their achievements, do not give up, but persevere, and eventually, with encouraging gestures and words, they will gain confidence. How we engage in conversation with children will influence the evidence we receive. Think about how we feel as adults when we are in conversation with someone who fails to listen and is distracted or uninterested. Show the child how important their conversation is, give eye contact, make gestures, smile, nod and show you are listening and that you are interested in what they have to say.

Oral evidence provides more detailed and reliable information than that which is written at this early stage of development. Children's capacity to think and understand far outweighs their skill in interpreting it in written form (Fisher 2004). When studying the way children develop, Vygotsky placed great importance on the role of speech and the social nature of children; he placed importance on dialogue between children and their social world, placing more emphasis on the social process and how it shapes individual development (Slee and Shute 2003).

We can learn a great deal from studying how children learn and communicate in the home environment. As first educators, we recognise the importance of parents in the learning process and their contribution to children's assessment. Tizzard and Hughes were interested in exploring the quality of children's conversations at home and at school. They concluded that often the richer forms of conversation happened in the home environment when children were employed in spontaneous activities in which one or both participants were engaged. They felt this was so, because of the meaningful context in which children learn. Parents naturally chat with their child during everyday events, washing the dishes, making the beds, and preparing meals, and this conversation will often bear little or no relevance to the task in which they are involved. This is something you can build upon when planning for experiences in your own setting, creating opportunities for spontaneous conversation and learning to happen side by side (Tizzard and Hughes, cited in Fisher 2004).

Children's conversations reveal their needs and interests. Babies' earliest form of communication is made through 'crying' to attract the attention of an adult and quickly develops to smiles, gurgles and screams as they delight in two-way communication, encouraged by the words and gestures they receive in response. In settings, practitioners continue to celebrate children's achievements in their learning and reaching significant milestones such as birthdays. These may be stickers or certificates awarded in class or whole-school assemblies, as a shared celebration with others. By doing this, we raise their levels of self-esteem and can significantly benefit their overall motivation to learn.

To feel secure and have confidence in entering into self-assessment tasks, it is up to you to make positive responses to their efforts and ideas, not heap them with empty and often quite meaningless praise. The overuse of stickers and throw-away comments such as 'well done' or 'good boy/girl' can become meaningless, unless the reason for their award be clearly communicated, inviting joint discussion of

Figure 5.1 Thumbs up and down self-assessment

and agreement with their personal achievement. A successful strategy for this is when children are invited to make thumbs up or thumbs down self-assessment at the end of a learning experience that indicates their level of understanding. Their response can be captured on a photo or noted as information on tick list assessments (Figure 5.1).

Children should be invited to contribute to their personal record of achievement or learning journey by making choices for the evidence that is inserted and be invited to comment on others. This is a form of using both self and peer assessment in small groups and provides valuable experience for children in taking decisions on each other's learning and recognising and celebrating achievement.

Making opportunities for assessment

Remember that children learn from everything, even things you have not planned for, such as a fall of snow (DCSF 2008c: 3.1). With this in mind, it is really important that within your weekly timetable you make opportunity for spontaneous learning experiences such as an unexpected change in the weather or an object one of the

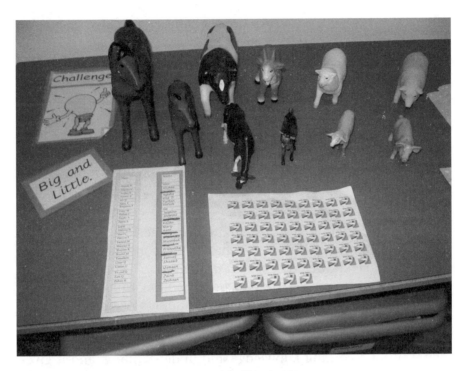

Figure 5.2   Self-assessment task to classify animals

children has found on their way to the setting that can be shared with everyone and enjoyed by all.

The EYFS documentation is very clear that the dominant method of assessing achievement and progress should be by looking at what children are doing. In Figure 5.2, you can see an example of a self-assessment activity that encourages children to make independent decisions about their understanding and learning. They are able to record their involvement in the activity, share their learning with an adult, and reward themselves with stickers, should they believe they successfully completed the task.

Each week several challenge tasks are set up in the classroom. This task involved children in a sorting activity that challenged them to organise the animals into two distinct sets according to their size, big or small. A class list was on the table next to the animals and children were instructed to make their own record to show they had completed the task successfully. This was done by looking for their name on the class list and placing a tick next to it. Once this was completed, children could then select a sticker as reward for their challenge. The results of this task are shared in the weekly team meeting and inform children's learning journeys, allowing practitioners to plan for next steps.

> **🔑 Key Point**
>
> - On your weekly timetable, plan for time to talk to children to enter into self-assessment activities.

Wells (1986) believed that it is the willingness on the part of the teacher to negotiate that gives children confidence to explore their own understandings. Knowledge has to be constructed afresh by each individual knower. Assessment tasks need to be open-ended and should offer children a variety of opportunities to explore, experiment, investigate and hypothesise. Practitioners need to encourage children to take risks in secure and safe environments, so there are no right answers or predicted outcomes. Children can devise their own ways of recording knowledge and understanding, and if given opportunity to do this, they will select ways that make sense to them and give all the information they want to share. What follows is an example of how one practitioner recognised that children often create their own effective method of self-assessment, and an explanation of how this evidence was presented. As a result of following child-led choices for play, a fantasy princess box was introduced. After playing happily for some time with the contents of the box, Praneetha and Mary Anne went to the mark-making table and produced the drawings shown in Figures 5.3 and 5.4. Their individual explanations of their drawings were recorded by the practitioner and carefully used for assessment purposes.

Praneetha proudly presented her illustration (Figure 5.3) to the practitioner who praised her creativity. The practitioner enthusiastically engaged in conversation with her, encouraging Praneetha to talk about her picture, and this was the explanation she gave:

> This is a prince now this is going to be a princess next. This is the house for the princess. This is a bus with a pig flying.

The detail that was shared here presents an insight into Praneetha's current understanding of the concept of princesses and fairy tales. It offers the practitioner clear assessment evidence that she can identify fairy story characters and put them into familiar context, as she

Figure 5.3   Nursery Class: Drawing by Praneetha, aged 4 years and 2 months

speaks about the house for her two characters. She is also developing understanding of imaginary context as she continues to extend her story to include the flying pig.

Mary Anne enjoyed talking about her drawing (Figure 5.4) and explained:

Figure 5.4   Nursery Class: Drawing by Mary Anne, aged 3 years and 7 months

I'm drawing a castle. This is a road, this is a house, this is another road to this house [she turned over the page and drew a person]. She's upside down. She's a dippy girl, oh! She's a Barbie, a Barbie playing with a ball.

Positive assessment was made about this drawing and Mary Anne's explanation. An understanding of story context was demonstrated as she spoke about castles, houses and roads. By identifying Barbie as a name for her character, she clearly demonstrated she was able to use prior knowledge and play experiences and use elements of this to extend her learning even further. She chose the Barbie character and confidently introduced her into her story context, showing her developing ability to enter into creative storytelling. The two girls were clearly interested in princesses, and their enthusiasm for this theme challenged them to make further independent choices for their learning. They extended their own unique ideas and personal understanding in the mark-making area through creative drawing and meaningful explanation.

Reflective Activity

How do you know that you listen to all children?

- Create your own formats for recording information that can be easily shared with children, parents and the team.
- Look at a typical timetable for the week. Think about how you can make time to enter into meaningful talk with children.

Barriers to accessing meaningful assessment

It is equally important that, when you ask questions of children, you are not demanding answers to things that you already know. Children are very aware as to whether practitioners' questions are genuine. Below is an example of such a situation, which occurred between an experienced Foundation Stage teacher in a Reception class and a 4-year-old boy. It gives a real example of the importance of planning meaningful activities matched to children's level of understanding and perception.

Many years ago I was teaching a Reception class in a large, inner-city primary school. As part of their writing task, I would ask the children to copy their name and address from a card that I had produced to enable me to settle the children on the task. However, one day David refused to comply with the task. I asked him, 'Why aren't you writing your address?' He replied, 'Why do I have to write it? I don't need to!' Thinking I had the answer, I said, 'If you get lost, you will be able to tell someone where you live.' 'David replied, 'I'll just find a policeman.' This really made me think about the underlying purpose of tasks that we offer children and how they have to be meaningful to them. As a result of this experience, I never insisted that they write their address again, unless they wanted to. This example clearly shows that in order to produce good-quality writing, children need to be motivated and have a reason to write – that is, writing for a purpose. David saw no reason why he should write his name when he could simply tell the practitioner, and, more importantly, he was able to offer a meaningful strategy for a problem. A further question to consider is, when we ask children to record their learning, do they feel limited by their capacity to record or draw? They may experience barriers to making successful responses, because of a lack of understanding as to how to complete the task or worksheet. This is often evident when children complete Standard Assessment Tests (SATs) at the end of both Key Stages 1 and 2. A failure to achieve predicted levels of attainment for some children can be related to the way the question is presented in the test. Had it been organised in a more familiar way, they quite possibly would have given an accurate answer. The layout of a page, the size of a text box, or even the symbol we expect them to draw, can inhibit their opportunity to be successful. You need to use prior assessment of their skills to inform your self-assessment design.

An example of this is recorded in Figure 5.5, which shows a student's design for a self-assessment tool that was created for her least-able group of learners on school placement. She discovered that her original idea for pupil self-assessment which challenged children to record their specific learning in continuous provision areas was proving difficult for this group and as such did not provide a true assessment of what they could actually do. She researched a simplified model idea on a popular website and then created her own template, based upon her prior knowledge of their unique way of learning and skill in recording effectively. The design she created required children to tick the appropriate statement that reflected their achievement. Her later evaluations of pupil assessment outcomes demonstrated that this offered her a more successful tool for self-assessment.

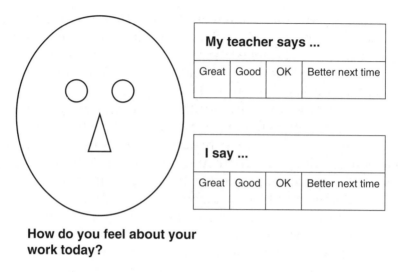

My teacher says ...			
Great	Good	OK	Better next time

I say ...			
Great	Good	OK	Better next time

How do you feel about your work today?

Figure 5.5   Smiley face self-assessment

Practitioners need to ensure that no more than 20 per cent of the total evidence for the EYFSP is gained from adult-directed activity. The remainder of the evidence should be drawn from knowledge of the child, observations and anecdotal assessments (QCA 2008: 10).

Children's ability to self-assess learning

To enable children to make confident self-assessments, it is essential they display a certain level of positive self-esteem. When children are engaged in making decisions about their learning and how they achieved, it adds to their self-esteem. If they only ever receive judgements from adults, they will not learn the critical life skill of self-motivation.

It is therefore important that children are supported in the skill to self-reflect and are invited to consider the following:

• What interests me?

• What do I enjoy doing?

• What do I want to be able to do?

- What helps me to learn?

- What would I like to know?

As adults we can support children in this personal skill, getting them to use their own initiative, and to make personal decisions by taking part in exciting and motivating problem-solving tasks. One such experience that I encouraged was whilst working with children in a Reception class who were enthralled by the building development that was happening at that time in the school grounds. I arranged to have a supply of building materials such as sand, cement and bricks delivered to our outdoor provision. We made good relationships with the workmen on site, who supplied us with a number of tools, including spades, trowels and a wheelbarrow for the children to use. They were thrilled on arriving at the setting that first morning and busily engaged in building an area as a garage for our wheeled toys. New skills were emerging each day as children explored mixing mortar and cementing bricks together to build walls, alongside planning and measuring their design. The activity was simple to organise and provided real-life, meaningful experiences that engaged the children and presented wonderful assessment as they chatted happily together, supported by practitioners taking decisions and supporting one another through new learning and skills. We used circle time as a tool for self-assessment, giving all children opportunity to speak about their activities and experiences in the outdoor area. Their ideas were recorded on to Post-it notes, which were easily transferred to personal records of achievement. We also used video recordings of outdoor activity that we later viewed with the children, inviting their comments and explanations as to what they remembered about specific events and what they believed they had learned.

Key Point

- Model the art of making self-assessment to scaffold children's understanding.

Making self-assessment presents children with an opportunity to reflect on their learning and contribute their ideas. Over time, creative ideas emerge for classroom practice, which range from simple

GOOD NEWS!

Today, _____ accomplished the following:

(name)

Signed, _____

Figure 5.6   Good News template: share a recordable event

practitioner-designed formats to more refined models that use technology such as 'voting pads' and software programmes.

We have included an example of a useful self-assessment format (Figure 5.6) that challenges children to regularly record their experiences. For those who have not yet developed mark-making skills, their ideas can be personally illustrated and annotated by a supportive adult.

The good news templates can be added to a central wall display to be viewed and enjoyed by children and parents too. Copies can be made and added to learning journeys, and as more and more are collected, a lovely idea is to transfer them to a large book that can be enjoyed and shared with children in the reading area.

Case Study: Nursery class: 3–4 years old

Another example of children using self-assessment is recorded in the following case study which happened in a nursery class with a group of children aged between and 3 and 4 years.

Children are encouraged each week to actively engage in specific challenges, and their achievements are recorded and duly rewarded as they occur. On Fridays we name our Star of the Week, who is selected as a result of a particular personal achievement during that week. This child is able to take the class cup home for the weekend along with a certificate to celebrate the achievement. James was at the mark-making table holding a pencil in his left hand and was attempting to write his name. He turned to Ben, who was sitting next to him, and said, 'When I can write my name all by myself, then I'll be Star of the Week and I'll take the trophy home!'

James had clearly developed his own ideas of what he thought he had to do to become Star of the Week and was working on achieving his goal. He was practising fine motor skills as he engaged in play in the mark-making area that he believed would assist him in successfully writing his name. He was motivated and his self-esteem was high.

There are very important reasons why encouraging children to self-assess can be of value both to them and to practitioners.

Self-assessment

Self-assessment is important because it

- Enables children to have an element of control over their own learning environment.

- Gives children a sense of responsibility and self-esteem.

- Gives opportunities for real-life problem-solving experiences.

- Enables the teacher to see things from the children's perspective.

To engage children in purposeful self-assessment, it is really important that they be reminded of what it is they are assessing, and how to do this successfully. This can be achieved by displaying questions and prompt cards in continuous provision areas, which must be regularly communicated and supported by adults, to encourage children to enter into the process of self-review.

The kinds of questions that can be displayed could be:

- Do I know what I want to achieve?

- What have I learnt today?

- How did I do it?

A typical activity to engage children in self-assessment is to encourage them to think about their learning experience. One successful way of doing this is to ask targeted questions of children. The answers below were given by children in response to the question, 'What do you think helps you to learn?' Here are some of the answers that children gave:

- Friends.

- My brain.

- Playing.

- Play dough.

- My head.

This group of children were questioned quite informally by the practitioner during periods of child-initiated play in the continuous provision areas. Their answers interestingly offer an array of explanations which provide a snapshot as to their cognitive understanding about how they learn. These ideas can be explored further with each child, in order to fully understand their rationale for such responses and help the practitioner gain a greater insight into this self-assessment.

⚿ Key Point

- Explore creative ideas for self-assessment on websites, in books, and by talking to other members of staff.

Peer-assessment

Child-initiated learning in the early years offers a perfect opportunity to extend the practice of peer assessment. The EYFS profile states:

> Much evidence will be gleaned from daily interactions with individuals and
> groups of children, as practitioners build up their knowledge of what children
> know and can do .... This is demonstrated most effectively when children are
> engaged in self initiated activities. (QCA 2008: 9)

Peer assessment is a great tool to raise self-esteem and encourage
children to gain confidence in speaking about their ideas and opin-
ions.This can be easily integrated into practice by inviting children
to contribute and share ideas for future planning and activities,
which are fuelled by their personal interests and experiences.
Children can also make decisions about learning spaces and organi-
zation, and this can be encouraged by sorting and labelling resources,
deciding upon where they should be located, and naming work
areas. It is important that children be invited to contribute to their
learning experiences, as this will contribute to their overall motivation to learn. Effective practitioners seize opportunities to involve
children in planning for future learning and share their knowledge
about children at weekly team meetings. Children's personal assessment about what they enjoy doing and their unique skills can be
readily used to inform future planning and experiences.

> Adults are aware of children's interests and understandings and the adults
> work together to develop an idea or a skill. (DCSF 2008a: 1.28)

A good example of this happening effectively in practice was shared
by a practitioner in a children's centre. She explained how, at the end
of each term, the children are gathered together and invited to contribute their ideas for new learning experiences. It was during one of
these sessions that a number of children, four boys, were eager to
talk about a story they had obviously enjoyed, 'Pete the Pirate', that
had been shared with them in an earlier activity. They were so
enthused by the idea of finding treasure that the team of practitioners realised the importance of capturing this enthusiasm and decided
to use the theme of pirates for the next term's learning. Children
engaged in a thought shower activity that challenged their current
understanding and knowledge of pirates. This allowed practitioners
to make an accurate assessment of children's range of experiences and
ideas relating to pirates and so use them to plan meaningful next steps
in learning.

Figure 5.7 shows an example of the thought shower activity based
upon the theme of pirates. Everything the children contributed was
recorded and transferred on to this template, and informed both
adult-led and child-initiated learning opportunities for the following
term. Practitioners thoughtfully planned new challenges based upon

Planning from Children's Interests

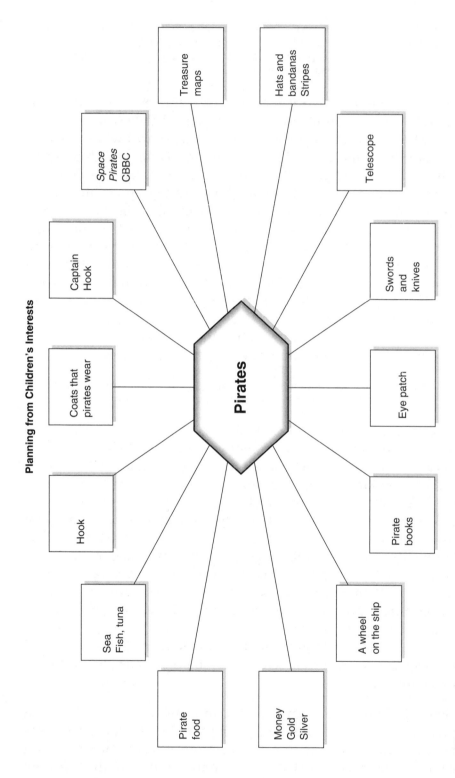

Figure 5.7 Pirate spider diagram

prior knowledge of pupil assessment. They were keen to further motivate the four boys and creatively plan appropriate learning challenges to interest the whole group.

Alexander et al. researched the effective use of whole-class practice in encouraging self and peer assessment in Key Stage 2; however, Siraj-Blatchford et al. (2002) dismissed the use of these forms of assessment, claiming that they are ineffective in early years. A very good example of this is often witnessed in circle time activity, where many children are seen to simply repeat what others have said before them, in response to practitioner questioning.

However, a more effective use of whole-class assessment is that of the plenary where children are invited to review their learning alongside practitioner and peers. In this practice, children realise that they will regularly review the learning experience and it will be evaluated by an audience. This practice mirrors the international 'High/Scope' approach to active learning, when children enter into a process of plan–do–review, believed to encourage self-discipline and a positive attitude towards completing tasks satisfactorily for their own sake, rather than for the practitioners. In a similar way, the plenary offers children the opportunity to attach language to their practical experiences, which encourages them to be more conscious of their actions and more likely to refer to them in later learning. It also presents great opportunity for children to peer-assess the achievements of their friends by making positive comments and sharing their thoughts with a wide audience.

> As children enter into sustained shared thinking they learn through talking, recalling, evaluating and learning from experiences, being able to build upon what they have done and so drawing on this for future learning. (DCSF 2008c: 4.3)

The key message here is recognising the importance of allowing children adequate time to talk about experiences as they play, and is clearly demonstrated in the following example.

Sarah and Amy were in the workshop area, making stars. Sarah said, 'I've got lots of stars at my house.' Amy said, 'I've spread all the glue out. Now I'm putting these sparkles on' (in the spangles were some stars). Sarah then said, 'I want some stars on mine.' Amy replied, 'I've got two stars. Here's one.' Sarah gave a star to Amy. Amy then placed her hand in the tub of spangles and let them trickle through her fingers. Sarah said 'Now these spangles will tickle.' Amy replied, 'I'm taking my star home. It's good.' 'Me too,' said Sarah.

This conversation reflects a shared learning experience. It includes examples of supportive language and meaningful dialogue between the two that challenge and extend personal ideas and move the activity in a new direction. The children draw on their mathematical knowledge while enjoying this sensory experience. Their conversation and language indicate their cognitive understanding of how this learning may be perceived by an adult. They are both eager to take the stars home and share their newly found experience with their parents.

This chapter aimed to show you the importance of including children's own voices and their ideas in making assessment. It has communicated simple ideas practitioners can employ in supporting children in engaging in self and peer assessment activities that offer essential records of assessment to plan more meaningful personalised next steps for learning.

Further Reading

Palmer, S. (2005) *Toxic Childhood*. London: Orion.

- Offers interesting examples about the way children and adults perceive childhood in the 21st century. The discussion presents some thought provoking ideas about the way we listen to children and what they tell us.

Dunkin, D. (2001) *Thinking Together: Quality Adult: Child Interactions*. New Zealand Council for Educational Research.

- Great ideas in understanding the way children think and how adults can prepare for meaningful conversation with children.

Carr, M. (2001) *Assessment in Early Childhood Settings*. London: Paul Chapman.

- Interesting ideas about developing learning stories for useful assessment practice.

Useful Websites

www.surestart.gov.uk

- This offers very useful information for those who work with children 0–5 years of age about current government initiatives, advice and support for parents.

www.tinyurl.com/yjmymv

- This gives advice on giving children a voice.

6

Collecting meaningful evidence

Denise Chadwick and Anne Webster

Chapter Objectives

- To understand the various forms of evidence that enable practitioners to make informed judgements about individual children's stages of development and plan for appropriate next steps for learning.

This chapter explores the importance of accessing and recording evidence of children's learning and skills as a way of helping practitioners effectively meet the needs of children in their care. It considers the many forms of evidence that can be collected and the range of partners that contribute to the ongoing holistic records of children's achievement and learning. It explores how evidence can be used to inform parents of their child's progress and assist practitioners in planning for future learning. Discussion will also be included to understand how practitioners link with other agencies that are part of the children's workforce. The literature draws on key early years research, such as the EPPE report, in understanding the rationale for making ongoing pupil observation to inform records of achievement.

Why collect evidence?

If we are to meet individual needs we have to make an accurate and holistic assessment of what children can do. From the day they are born, assessments are made that detail personal statistics about the

Figure 6.1   Photograph of the Red Book

baby that make every child unique. Records will be made about important physical assessment, such as gender and size, that inform their individual record. This data is now recorded in one document known as a red book (Figure 6.1) that includes important guidance to support new parents in understanding children's milestones and stages of development. The red book also lists ongoing medical records and immunisations that children will require in the early years of their life.

Individual records are regularly updated by health professionals who have contact with the child and carer. These could include health visitors, doctors, childminders and pre-school workers. This evidence will form the earliest record of development as children move on to early years settings. Once evidence is gathered it is used in a number of ways to contribute to organisation and aspects of teaching and learning. Professionals are responsible for collecting and collating regular and ongoing assessments of children's learning and performance in order to plan for the next steps.

> Ongoing assessment is an integral part of the learning and development process. Providers must ensure that practitioners are observing children and responding appropriately to help them make progress from birth towards the early learning goals. (DCSF 2008c: 2. 2.19)

Children's records, or learning journeys as they are now known, need to be regularly reviewed and updated in order to maximise every opportunity to support children in meeting the five outcomes of *Every Child Matters* (DFES 2004). These learning journeys offer a meaningful record of evidence that will inform the Early Years Foundation Stage Profile (EYFSP), a summative assessment report which is completed at the end of the Foundation Stage.

Practitioners will need to;

- Review the information that has been collected and note any gaps in learning or skills.

- Make holistic assessment of a child's progress and development.

- Draw planning points together; it is important that long-term as well as short-term changes are recorded.

There should also be planned opportunity to review and discuss children's records with the team, who should:

- Review all records where possible once per half-term and a minimum of once per term.

- Review assessment records more frequently if staffing ratios allow more regular assessments to be undertaken.

- Ensure that assessments are moderated to check the quality and parity of team decisions.

 Reflective Activity

Think about the kind of evidence you can collect that will offer a broad range of information about children's holistic development. Where will it come from and what should it tell you about the unique child?

(Continued)

- Insert evidence into a learning journey document; make sure you clearly annotate any photographs or children's work to show their achievement and stage of development.
- Plan the next steps for personalised learning and development in each area of learning.

⊙━ Key Point

- Plan for weekly team discussions to share evidence, and display the timetable in a central place.

Effective practice and joined-up working

The overarching aim of the new EYFS framework is to help young children achieve the five outcomes of the *Every Child Matters* (ECM) agenda. The EYFS promotes a holistic approach to the process of making assessments of children. The document has been organised to strengthen partnerships with parents and children's services, and it communicates the importance of multi-agency working. Multi-agency working underpins the *Every Child Matters* agenda and informs the principles and practice of the EYFS.

> The Common Assessment Framework (CAF) enables effective communication between the various agencies involved with children who have additional needs, or a child about whom there are concerns. (DCSF 2008c: 2.14)

Ensuring that effective practice is achieved in the context of working with other professionals and agencies that are outside the setting is one of the key principles in the new curriculum documentation. Anning and Edwards (Palaiologou 2008) speak of a 'joined-up approach, by professionals who work together as part of a multi-agency team. The desire to make sure that children are accessing the support, protection and care they are entitled to is also clearly defined in the Children Act 2004.

Similarities exist between the New Zealand approach to early years education and the EYFS framework in the UK. One example of this can be seen in the approach to achieving effective joined-up working between education and health. The term 'educare' is now embedded in current policy in the UK early years ethos and refers to provision that endows education and care with equal status. It underpins the importance of the professional working within a multi-agency framework, thus building close links with alternative agencies of the children's workforce. This joined-up approach between agencies is now clearly embedded in New Zealand. Since 2003, the Ministry of Education have developed positive strategies to achieve integrated working between health, education and social care (Farquhar 2003).

Importance is placed on continuity and communication with all agencies that are involved with children and families. Steps can be taken to ensure that effective partnership working is achieved at key points of transition. It is important that practitioners should:

- Establish visits between pre-school and early years settings to build links and establish familiar practice and routines.

- Develop meaningful recording formats that gather essential information in preparation for the point of transition.

- Hold regular cluster meetings with pre-school provision; share curriculum content and approach to learning, information formats, and record keeping structures.

- Hold joint training sessions to focus on key areas of defined training needs and sharing innovative practice.

Central to all effective partnership working is the 'Common Core of Skills and Knowledge' (CWDC 2007), which supports all practitioners in creating a joined up workforce to deliver the five outcomes of *Every Child Matters*:

- Being healthy.

- Staying safe.

- Enjoying and achieving.

- Achieving economic well–being.

- Making a positive contribution.

The Common Core of Skills and Knowledge includes clear statements, which define key skills that are required by professionals when collecting information about children and young people, in order to successfully deliver the five outcomes. Under the second heading of the Common Core Skills entitled 'Child and Young Person' is a section dedicated to the role of observation and judgement. It is suggested that in order to work effectively in a professional role with children and young people we need to be competent and confident in the following specific skills:

- Understand that babies, children and young people see and experience the world in different ways.

- Observe a child or young person's behaviour, understand its context, and notice any unexpected changes.

- Record observations in an appropriate manner.

- Evaluate each situation, taking into consideration individuals and their circumstances and development issues.

- Make considered decisions on whether concerns can be addressed by providing or signposting additional sources of information or advice.

- Be able to recognise the signs of a possible developmental delay.

- Listen actively and respond to concerns expressed about developmental or behavioural changes.

- Be able to support children and young people with a developmental difficulty or disability, and understand that their families, parents and carers will also need support and reassurance.

- Where you feel support is needed, know when to take action yourself and when to refer to managers, supervisors or other relevant professionals.

- Be able to distinguish between fact and opinion. (Palaiologou 2008)

Although not exhaustive, the above list offers a comprehensive checklist of the essential skills of the early years professional. It aims to highlight the important role of the practitioner in making early identification and assessment of children's needs.

So what kinds of evidence do we collect at the earliest point of transition into settings? When parents first seek places for early years provision, they are usually asked to complete an application form with targeted questions about their child, such as date of birth, home address, place of birth, names of parents or carers, and names of other siblings. Information about personal interests, likes and dislikes is also collected, which can then inform planning and teaching.

Home visits

One of the first forms of evidence and communication that is made between settings and new admissions will be accessed during a home visit. This is prior to admission, when one or more members of the early years team visit the child in their own home. Information that is recorded here will be through discussion with the parent or carer and will contribute to the child's future personal record of achievement or learning journey. Many settings create their own documentation in preparation for such visits in order to gather the meaningful information they require. This evidence is filed as part of the personal record of achievement and used as a point of reference by the team of practitioners working with the child and the family.

Figure 6.2 shows an example of a typical format with suggested headings to enable practitioners to gather key information at home visits and during the transition period.

Admissions and points of transition

New admissions usually enter settings through an organised transition period, when both the child and the parent will be invited to visit for short periods of time. It is a further opportunity for informal discussion and provides another access point for greater information about the child's unique experiences and skills. Often information is shared that offers a more holistic picture of the child. Together they may talk about home and family structures. Perhaps a new baby or a recent family bereavement will impact upon children's ability to make a smooth transition into the setting or present longer-term implications for learning. This will require personalised action plans and need to be shared with the team to provide appropriate support for the child and family.

Record of Home Visit and Transition Week One

Home visit	Questions and prompts		
Name: Home Language:			
Date: Observation Any Additional Information	About the child: Are they interested in our presence? Do they stay close to parent/carer? Is the child relaxed, animated, shy etc. Relationship with parent/carer	Do they have good mobility and balance? Are they able to play independently? Do they use language effectively? What do they enjoy doing? Any specific needs?	
Transition week Date:			
Observation and Comments	Action and Next Steps		Signature
Day 1			
Day 2			
Day 3			
Day 4			
Day 5			

Figure 6.2   Format for home visit and week one transition

When children arrive from earlier pre-school experiences, their record of learning and development should be forwarded to the next provider. This will enable practitioners to plan for personalised need and identify the next steps in learning. These should be carefully matched to accurate records of what children can already do.

Parents or carers of children who arrive in the UK from other countries or simply relocate in the UK, will be required to present records of health or prior educational assessment if their children have attended pre-school settings such as childminders, playgroups or nursery. Difficulty is often experienced however when children arrive in the UK from other countries, as a result of language barriers, cultural differences, or the quality and usefulness of the available records. To ensure that children's needs are met, it is imperative that accurate records showing date of birth and health checks are available to settings, and this is a key point of practice for multi-agency working across the children's services.

> Practitioners will frequently need to work with professionals from other agencies to meet needs and use their knowledge and advice to provide children's social care. (DCSF 2008a: 10)

In school settings, a number of 'admission places' are set aside for priority places; these are often accessed by children who are part of disadvantaged families or may already be involved with other children's services, such as health or social services. The number of available priority places is determined by numbers on roll and is currently allocated as three places for every 26 children. If families are known to children's services, there should be detailed records of the nature of their involvement, outlining any support that has been provided, which are then forwarded to the next setting. It is usually the head teacher or setting manager who is given initial access to this information, and it is essential that this be shared with the early years team. This good practice enables them to prepare for personalised future learning and development and to plan for continuity built upon earlier assessment. The team will also begin to establish early links with parents and carers in order to forge positive partnerships. Evidence is collected from a range of partners involved with the child. These will include parents and carers, early years practitioners senior management, siblings, extended family members, wider school staff such as lunchtime organisers, crossing patrol attendant, etc.

Parent partnerships

It is important that a number of people contribute to the learning journey, as this offers a more holistic range of evidence about the child from different perspectives. Parents are seen as first educators in children's lives, and their contribution to their children's future is recognised by those in early education. The overall responsibility for collecting evidence of children's learning should be a shared effort from a range of partners. Luff (Palaiologou 2008) believes that observation, collecting and documentation should have a supportive role in children's learning and in the professionals' practice. It should not be simply a paper exercise, but must add to the value of an educational programme and be beneficial to children's assessment (cited in Palaiologou 2008).

Parental involvement therefore should be far more than signing a consent form or accepting an invitation to a parents' evening. Their involvement should be given a high profile and seen as a key part in the overall effectiveness of gathering evidence of their child's development. It is thought that engaging them in initial discussions when observations are designed is a useful strategy to both equip and empower parents to take a responsible role in the overall responsibility of children's care and education. Early years research has shown that when parents are involved in early years practice and activities from the start of the observation process, there is greater chance of achieving close collaboration – they can become helpful collaborators (Sylva et al. 2004).

So how are these kinds of partnerships achieved? We firmly believe that, in order to establish effective partnership practice, expectations of success should be high. But it is equally important for practitioners, parents and carers to be realistic and ready to accept different levels of partnership working. Try as we may, sometimes achieving high-level partnership working, for all children in our care, may be less successful than we had initially hoped. Parents present settings with unique personal circumstances and have varied expectations for both their children's learning and their personal involvement. It is important that practitioners respect and recognise this individuality and, whenever possible, design creative parent partnerships that match their needs as well as supporting the shared interest in their child.

An essential quality of professional practice in the children's workforce is to have the desire, determination and passion to work effectively in partnership with parents. Through our vocation, we choose to improve the lives of children in our care, and accepting anything less than high standards for practice should never be a conscious part of our vision.

In 2003, the Ministry of New Zealand introduced their new approach to early childhood education, which was defined as from birth to 5 or 6 years of age. They believed that building partnerships between schools and families was more than just simply listening to each other. They termed it 'A joint construction of outcomes and pathways' (Farquhar 2003).

To establish clear partnership ethos and working, it is essential that parents be treated with respect from the earliest meeting. Positive partnership working is achieved through clear channels of communication that enable information sharing to be achieved. Parents should be informed not only of their child's well-being and progress, but also of future events in the setting and any important changes to provision. This should be a two-way process; they, too, need to be able to pass information to the setting and know it will be acknowledged and respected.

To engage parents in the process of observation in the home environment, it is essential that practitioners support them in understanding the objectives of this process. We should not assume that they will have a good understanding of the purpose of making observations of their children at play – why should they? It is our responsibility to guide and support them not only in learning how to make quality observation, but also, and more importantly, to understand why observation and assessment are so important. This can be achieved through a series of planned induction meetings between the parent or carer and the setting. Specific information about observation can be shared in an understandable and non-threatening way, and it will focus upon:

- Sharing clear information as to the purpose of observation. What is it for? Why is it important to daily practice? How will it benefit the educational programme?

- How does observation assist practitioners in meeting children's needs and how does it inform future activities?

- Parents need very clear guidelines as to what to observe and how to record their observations; share examples of the formats we suggest they could use. Model the practice of observing and recording.

- We as practitioners need to be aware of meeting the needs of those parents who may have low level literacy skills, have English as an additional language, or lack confidence in recording. Place alternative methods of making observation their way, such as the use of cameras and video clips.

- We need to clearly communicate their right to access all observations made on their child; their involvement is their choice, and they have the right to withdraw at any time.

Sometimes practitioners are sceptical about the information they gain from parents, as the latter often perceive children in a different way from how practitioners see them in settings. This information, however, is of great importance, as it presents key information about holistic development and gives us invaluable information about how they behave in the home environment. Parents need to be assured that practitioners recognise that they are the ones who know their children best. Below is an example of how one practitioner approached a parent for ideas and advice about their child.

 Case Study: Children's centre, Sam, aged 3 years and 7 months

Read the following case study and think about the importance of making accurate pupil assessment that is informed through ongoing observation of a pupil's learning and communication with parents and carers.

After observing Sam for several weeks, I was concerned about the development of his speech and language. Sam was always running after the other children and shouting loudly at them. When I gained eye contact and engaged in conversation with him, his answers were mostly incoherent and loud. I decided to speak with his mum about my observations, and she subsequently informed me that Sam had an uncle who was deaf.

As a result of this conversation, I suggested that we refer Sam to the Speech and Language Therapy Service. Once he was assessed, both his parents and the school were presented with a report of their findings. Sam's results showed that he did indeed have below-average hearing. A language programme was put in place for him and he is now making good progress. If I had not approached Sam's mum, I am in no doubt that he would still be having problems and his ability to make good progress would have been seriously affected.

- Why do you think Mum had not noticed a possible issue here?
- What could you have done if Mum had not been willing to recognise that there may be a problem?

One of the earliest and best-known studies of parental involvement was made at Pen Green Early Excellence Centre in 1995. Parental involvement was encouraged by recording development at home in diaries and by using video cameras. As a result of this project, key findings about both the willingness of parents to be involved and the overall quality and effectiveness of their observations in supporting their practice were recorded:

- Some parents made insightful observations of children playing that informed nursery staff planning. Others simply recorded amusing incidents or family events such as weddings, birthday parties, etc.

- Many parents initially went for quantity rather than quality – parents were also eager for feedback, resulting in hours of video footage to be covered and unsustainable demands on staff.

It was decided that a number of strategies should be taken to improve the level of evidence and how parents make observations. Steps were taken to hold training sessions to assist parents in finding a focus for their observations and engaging parents and staff in a shared conceptual framework – 'a framework for thinking'. Staff believed that the way forward was to develop a shared language that could be used to discuss the ways children learn and review how adults can effectively intervene to support and extend learning (cited in Whalley 2008). Through this approach, parents are involved at the outset and are encouraged to take greater ownership of the process. It shows that they are valued contributors to the learning process and offers opportunity to raise their self-esteem and status.

> Play underpins all development and learning for young children. Most children play spontaneously, although some may need adult support, and it is through play that they develop intellectually, creatively, physically, socially and emotionally. (DCSF 2008c: 1.17)

As a way of structuring this 'framework for thinking', we have included a suggested format that could be used to achieve successful parent observation. We wanted to design something that would be

Would you like to share with us the things that you and your child like doing together.

reading - Milly likes to tell us a story from her books. She tells us one then we read to her.

Singing - Milly loves singing + music - more than TV!

Gardening - Milly loves playing in the garden with Fred. She loves snails - she calls them 'speccly!' She helps me weed + growing seeds etc.

Painting - Milly loves writing with everything. She pretends to make 'lists' etc!

Playing - 'making tea'.

Figure 6.3   Completed parent assessment format

simple to use and offer parents the opportunity to share aspects of their important experiences with their children. This was introduced in a nursery setting with overwhelming response from parents. Once the idea was clearly communicated, parents could access templates independently from the parents' display board, and completed forms were replaced in a similar way on a daily basis (Figure 6.3).

Taking decisions upon the information you want to collect and how to record it should be discussed with the whole team. When planning for observation, it is crucial that, in order to make quality and meaningful observations of children's learning and skills, the purpose of observing and how to do it need to be clearly understood by all those involved. Once agreed, it is the responsibility of the whole team to gather this information and contribute to the children's records. The final result should be collaborative, and not a single-effort product.

Effective teamwork in collecting evidence

Effective practitioners place the needs of the children at the forefront of their practice. However, it is of equal importance to achieve and sustain quality provision, and the needs of the team should also be given close consideration. When organising ways to collect evidence, it is essential that individual team members and respective roles be considered. The early years workforce brings a varied range of members; teacher, nursery nurse, and learning support assistant are but a few of the most familiar, and each presents a specific job description, with defined working hours and conditions. The task of managing such diverse teams requires considerable professional skill, demanding diplomacy, tact and understanding to establish the strategies and routines that meet the needs of the team.

Key decisions will need to be made as to how and when the team will access the information. Will observations be scheduled on weekly rotas to ensure that they happen? Often practitioners understand the importance of making and using observation to inform their assessment, but unless these are clearly planned for, other things take priority and opportunity to observe can be sidelined. Another important consideration for team consensus and clarity is in respect to their intentions for sharing and storing evidence. They need to explore and agree manageable structures for collecting and filing evidence, and timetable regular weekly opportunity to share key findings.

Key Points

- Always share ideas for new proformas or record keeping with the whole team prior to putting them into practice.
- How can we accommodate practitioners who may work part-time hours and have difficulty in attending weekly meetings? Many ideas have been tried and adapted by practitioners. It is through regular evaluation of practice by the whole team that the most successful methods are finally agreed. Some examples of good practice could be:
  - Jotting down notes in a notepad or on Post-it notes, which are placed into a central record-keeping document.
  - Using an evaluation box at the bottom of planning sheets to record any key points for learning; these are then shared at team discussion time.
  - Practitioners coding observations in a particular way to highlight the most important points to be noted.

This allows practitioners to have equal knowledge of children's levels of learning and skills, in order to plan well-informed next steps for their learning and make specific improvements for educational provision.

It is important that team members feel able to express their views and share their opinions, regardless of their status or team role. Making observation and taking judgements based upon the evidence we collect is a skilled process, but one that can be supported though effective training and mentoring. Just as children have individual personalities and skills, so, too, do the members of every team. Recognising individual skills and competencies, as well as supporting areas for development, has important implications not only for effective leadership of early years teams, but also for the provision of regular training opportunities matched to practitioner need:

- Whole-team training, focused training in how to observe and make assessments, and regular induction to support new team members.

- Important that they train together; this can be achieved though nominating training events linked to yearly, whole-school development planning.

- Carefully designed job descriptions, clearly outlining responsibilities; attending weekly team meetings; making observation; record keeping; and training and continued professional development.

Key Point

- At the start of each year, identify diary dates for team meetings and appraisals to review practice and share ideas.

Collecting the evidence

The role of the observation process for children and the educational programme should be to improve the quality, care and education that children receive, and to develop and enhance professional practice. Observations help practitioners to understand and reflect on the overarching and finer details of the educational programme, and, most importantly, they inform practitioners' understanding of the children in their care. An observation of learning can be made in any context or activity in which the child is engaged. Many observations of development are noticed quite incidentally as practitioners and parents go about their busy day, and do not always need to be planned. Recording information should therefore be simple, manageable and inform children's individual learning journeys. Childminders speak of having less opportunity to actively record observations but instead rely heavily on the verbal feedback they share with parents and carers on a day-to-day basis. Parents are, however, given a detailed written record of learning and development at the point of exit.

The Te Whariki approach to early years education in New Zealand presents an integrated approach that weaves observation into daily classroom activity. Margaret Carr also speaks about using observation to develop learning communities and using learning stories as a way of weaving this cultural ethos into daily practice (Carr 2001).

We believe that the concept of learning stories as explained by Margaret Carr presents some interesting and useful ideas that can be adapted quite easily to inform our own suggested early years assessment-learning. Her thoughts provide a successful, personalised approach to collecting evidence that draws upon a broad client base and interprets the evidence in a very creative and meaningful way.

The following section offers simple ideas for making and recording observation of learning. They are best suited to early years settings that involve a team of practitioners able to contribute to the whole process of assessment.

Catch as you can

These observations of children's learning are most easily recorded by scribbled evidence on Post-it notes, which are then transferred to their personal records of achievement. They can be collected at incidental times of any day when practitioners notice a child displaying an aspect of skill or learning. The most important thing to remember is to include the child's name and the date the observation was made. Further discussion about this information can take place at a later date to determine what achievement it may indicate and how to define the next steps (Figure 6.4).

Photographs

Seizing the moment and capturing children in action learning is great evidence of their achievement and skills. Photographs offer

Catch as you can observation

Date:

Name of child:

Look Listen Note: Observed learning:

Links to Development Matters:

Next steps:

Signature

Figure 6.4 Catch as you can recording format

Anna 14.1.09.

Anna matched (paired) the penguins 0 – 20. She said the number name in order matched + put them in the basket

Links with EYFS

PSRN NLC 4 5 6 7

Next steps Number programmes on I.WB to 20.

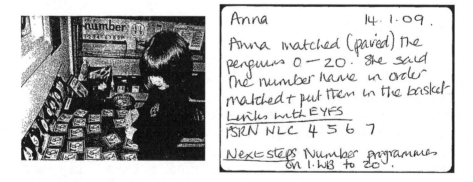

Figure 6.5 Photograph and annotated notes about Anna

accurate evidence of learning, which again should be dated and annotated, linking to the areas of learning and development in the EYFS, to show the specific learning that was achieved and the next steps (Figure 6.5).

Adult-focused or participant observations

These are usually recorded on a specific paper format, which defines the activity and learning objective. The information will record children's ability to meet the success criteria and in some cases take the learning to a further level. Such observations will be recorded during adult-led learning experiences or where the adult is playing alongside children in child-initiated play. Again it is essential that key information features on these records, including name, date, any specific learning needs, how learning was demonstrated, and suggested next steps for learning (Figure 6.6).

Parent and carer observations

Parents' and carers' contributions and their own assessment of their child's learning and development are equally important. Information from parents is often shared through direct conversation with practitioners, either informally day to day or at organised parent evenings. Many settings create simple recorded formats, which parents can complete and contribute to, about their involvement in their child's learning experience that again inform the 'learning journey'. A great example of parental involvement is using a 'Wow Wall' (Figures 6.7 and 6.8) as a focused display where parents are invited to record aspects of their child's achievements and make contributions to the display. This is also discussed in Chapter 8.

Children's self-assessments

Children should be given the opportunity to contribute to personal assessment and talk about their learning. Methods for successfully doing this are explained in greater detail in Chapter 5.

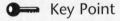 Key Point

- Make observation meaningful and manageable and timetable opportunities for making observation on your weekly timetable.

The underpinning rationale for observation and good record keeping is to enable early years teams, parents and children themselves to

Adult-Focused Observation

Activity:		Area of Learning:	
Date:		Cross-Curricular Links:	
Learning Challenge:			
Group Names:	Assessment Outcome:	Comments:	Next Steps:
Signature:			

Figure 6.6   Example of adult-focused format

Figure 6.7   Blank format for WOW wall

monitor progress and also to indicate specific points of evidence to inform the educational programme. Good record keeping should be continuous process that will provide evidence to support assessment and the wider educational provision. Many forms of record keeping are evident in practice, and include electronic records, such as spread-sheets and proformas, practitioner tick lists, scribbled notes, and

Figure 6.8   Photograph of WOW parent wall display board

numerous other creative forms of meaningful teacher assessments. So how, then, do accurate and meaningful records support our practice?

- They assist teams in meeting personalised provision for all children in order that they can experience developmental areas suggested by the EYFS.

- They help the team ensure continuity in early years practice.

- In sharing evidence, practitioners are encouraged to explore new and more creative pedagogies or experiences that will further enrich the educational programme.

- They provide evidence of communication with parents, other professionals and authorities.

- They encourage practitioners to be reflective in the way they support children and evaluative of their own performance.

Drummond (2003) believes that the role of professionals is to recognise the ultimate responsibility of their privileged position, to monitor the effects of their work, and to ensure that their good intentions for children are realised. We are in total agreement with this and consistently urge students to make regular reflection on their own learning, giving it equal importance to that of the children in their care (Drummond 2003, cited in Palaiologou 2008).

Further Reading

Hutchin, V. (1999) *Right From the Start. Effective Planning and Assessment in the Early Years.* London: Hodder and Stoughton.

- This offers an easy-to-read guide to making assessment of children's learning. It presents a range of simple, yet useful formats for collecting evidence.

Fisher, J. (2004) *Starting from the Child.* Buckingham: Open University Press.

- Gives meaningful examples of case study scenarios to support suggestions for effective practice.

Carr, M. (2001) *Assessment in Early Childhood Settings: Learning Stories.* London: Paul Chapman.

- An engaging text that will present food for thought about the concept of learning journeys as a tool for organising individual children's assessment.

Useful Websites

www.wiredforhealth.co.uk

- Up-to-date information on key aspects of children's health and well-being.

www.familylearning.org.uk

- Important site to review when considering elements of working with families.

www.peal.org.uk

- Lots of useful information about parents as partners in their children's learning.

7

Summarising learning and development at the end of the early years foundation stage

Jonathan Glazzard

Chapter Objectives

- To understand the use of the Early Years Foundation Stage Profile (EYFSP) as both a formative and summative assessment tool.
- To understand how the EYFSP works.
- To explore the contribution which parents or carers and children can make to the EYFSP.
- To consider ways of analysing profile data to enable practitioners to reflect on their own practice.

This chapter explains how the Early Years Foundation Stage Profile (EYFSP) (QCA 2008) works. It focuses on the key principle that both parents and children should be active agents in contributing to the profile, and the chapter also draws on case studies drawn from partner settings. This chapter will consider the use of the EYFSP as both a summative and formative assessment document. It also acknowledges the variation in practices that exist within different local authorities. We consider the profile to be a valuable record that can be used to inform teaching and learning throughout the final year of the Early Years Foundation Stage (EYFS). Additionally, the profile is an essential record of individual attainment, which must be valued by Year 1 practitioners if they are to effectively build on children's prior learning. This chapter addresses current policy, whereby profile data is closely scrutinised by schools, local authorities, and the Department for Children, Schools and Families (DCSF). National expectations of attainment for children at the end of the Foundation Stage are clearly defined, and schools and practitioners are required to justify teaching and outcomes within these settings.

Understanding the EYFSP

The profile is a **summative assessment** of children's attainment in all aspects of the six areas of learning at the end of the EYFS. In the profile the six areas of learning are made up of assessment scales. In some areas of learning, there may be more than one assessment scale. For example, personal, social and emotional development (PSED) is subdivided into three assessment scales. Each assessment scale carries a potential score of 9 scale points.

Scale points 1–3 are developmental and *must* be attained before scale points 4–8 can be awarded within each assessment scale. Scale points 1–3 indicate that a child is working towards the Early Learning Goals. Within a particular assessment scale, if a child achieves scale points 1–3, only the final total will be recorded as 3.

Scale points 4–8 are *not hierarchical* and can be achieved in any order. To award these scale points, a child must have been awarded scale points 1–3 first. Within any assessment scale, a total is awarded at the end of the Foundation Stage. For example, a child who has achieved scale points 4, 5 and 7 on a particular scale must have already achieved scale points 1–3 within the same assessment scale. Therefore the child's total score within this assessment scale would be 6. Practitioners should not record the highest scale point achieved as an overall total for any assessment scale. Instead they should total the number of scale points achieved. If a child has achieved scale points 1–4 and 6 within a particular assessment scale, the total score within that assessment scale will be 5, as five scale points have been achieved in total.

Scale point 9 can only be achieved in any assessment scale when a child has already achieved 8 scale points. Children attaining 9 scale points within an assessment scale would be working beyond the Early Learning Goals, and additional assessments and evidence to support judgements would be essential. Scale point 9 is inconsistent and in some assessment scales it equates to a child working within National Curriculum Level 1. However, in other assessment scales, scale point 9 describes a child working within National Curriculum Level 2. Practitioners need to be confident about their judgements, as scale point 9 indicates a child who is working within the expectations of the National Curriculum. It is recommended that all practitioners should be able to provide supporting documentation as evidence of the judgements they have made in relation to the EYFSP. This evidence could be in the form of photographic evidence, long and short observations of independent learning, audio evidence, samples of children's recorded work and video evidence. The evidence will have been collected over time as part of an ongoing process of formative assessment.

Key Point

- Complete the EYFSP in conjunction with tracking attainment against the EYFS framework. Judgements against the EYFS framework should inform judgements made on the EYFSP. Practitioners should refer to their bank of evidence collected through ongoing formative assessments to inform judgements about children's attainment against the profile.

The EYFSP summarises attainment at the end of the Foundation Stage but is also a valuable document in supporting Year 1 teachers to continue children's individual learning journeys. The profile data is a valuable tool to aid practitioners in the identification of individual, group and whole-class needs. In addition, it enables practitioners to identify weaknesses and strengths in the provision. The data is forwarded annually to the local authority. This in turn supports the local authority in evaluating the impact of early years provision on an authority-wide basis. This facilitates the identification of strengths and weaknesses within individual settings and groups of settings. The profile data enables local authorities to identify settings that require further support and aids local authority strategic planning. In turn, local authorities submit their data to the DCSF. This provides the government with national picture of the outcomes of teaching and learning in the EYFS.

Baseline profile data

Some settings elect to complete the profile only at the end of the EYFS. Other settings use the information gained from ongoing form-ative assessments to identify children's attainment against the profile scale points as an ongoing process throughout the final year of the Foundation Stage. This can be a very worthwhile process and can support practitioners in identifying individual, group and whole-class needs throughout the year.

From the beginning of the final year in the Foundation Stage, it is possible for children to attain profile scores in each assessment scale. These early judgements can be made on the basis of formative assess-ments that have been carried out in pre-school settings. This infor-mation should have been forwarded by *all* previous settings. Practitioners working in the final year of the Foundation Stage will need to confirm these judgements at the beginning of the academic year. For children with no pre-school experience, practitioners will need to spend the first few weeks of term carrying out initial baseline assessments against the EYFS framework. These early formative assessments can then be used to make early judgements about attain-ment in relation to the assessment scales on the profile.

This information provides the practitioner with a baseline on which to build attainment during the final year. This also helps practitioners to identify individual learning needs. Some children may have a very low profile score or no score at all on entry to the final year of the Foundation Stage. These children will need carefully considered sup-port to meet their learning needs. Additionally, this process will also aid in the identification of potentially gifted children or children working at higher developmental stages, who will need differentiated provision and extra challenge. Target groups are also easily identifiable and additional support should be planned to raise attainment for children working at lower stages of development. Some local authori-ties require settings to submit profile data on entry to the final year of Foundation Stage. This early data enables local authorities to monitor final outcomes against initial scores, and it enables practitioners and local authorities to evaluate the progress individuals and groups of learners have made.

Developing an ongoing record of attainment against the profile enables practitioners to support children further by involving parents and carers in their child's learning. Practitioners can identify *broad targets* to advance children's learning and these can be shared with parents. It is vital that practitioners and parents refer to both the framework and the profile. Broad targets can be identified from the profile. However, it is important to remember that *focused and achievable smaller steps in learning* are to be found in the EYFS framework. It is this framework that should always be the primary source for planning to meet children's individual learning needs and next steps.

Key Point

- Updating judgements against the EYFS framework and EYFSP should be an ongoing process. This aids practitioners in identifying individual next steps and the needs of groups of learners. This will also inform the practitioner of aspects of learning that may require further focus and aid in the identification of target groups.

Case Study: Kate: Reception class

Read the following case study and think specifically about the dangers and benefits of using the EYFSP in both a formative and summative way.

One local authority had conveyed a very strong message to practitioners over several years that all assessments and children's next steps in learning should be identified and planned with reference to the early years curriculum frameworks. Prior to 2008 and the implementation of the statutory EYFS framework, practitioners within this local authority referred to the *Curriculum Guidance for the Foundation Stage* (DfES 2000) for planning purposes. The same local authority stressed that the profile was purely a tool for summarising children's learning at the end of the Foundation Stage.

At the *beginning* of the academic year 2007–08, this authority was required to report profile scores in communication, language and literacy (CLL) and PSED for children who had just entered the final year of the EYFS. The purpose of this was to track individual attainment of children engaged in a synthetic phonics programme. This authority resisted the expectation that profile scores should be reported at this early stage and emphasised that the profile was a summative assessment of a child's learning. The resistance of this authority was to no avail. Therefore, practitioners had no choice but to begin to track children's progress against the profile scale points as well as against the framework *during* the final year of the Reception class.

Kate, although initially reluctant and supportive of the local authority's stance, quickly identified the advantages of tracking children's attainment against *both* the EYFS framework and the profile scale points. Kate was able to refer to assessments made against the framework to support her in identifying children's individual attainment against the profile and future learning needs throughout the year. However, now that she was also making judgements about children's learning throughout the year, she felt that it greatly enhanced her ability to identify individual attainment in specific aspects of learning for individual children. She was therefore able to identify broad targets for specific pupils and to plan interventions for those children who were at risk of attaining scores below national expectations. In addition, Kate found it easier to identify group needs and to target groups to support them in attaining national expectations in relation to the scale points. This process also effectively supported Kate in evaluating her own practice through the identification of areas for development in her own teaching.

- Do you think profile data is an effective way of helping practitioners to evaluate their practice in this way?
- What are the advantages of using the profile document in this way?
- What are the dangers of using the profile document in this way?

Key Point

- Spend valuable time confirming judgements made by previous settings. It is possible that children's attainment could have regressed during a vacation and practitioners therefore need to plan in frequent opportunities for assessment when the child enters the setting.

Making judgements against the EYFSP

Before awarding any scale point for any assessment scale, practitioners should consider the *moderated* evidence they have collected to support these judgements. It is essential that practitioners do not work in isolation and that scale points are awarded on the basis of ongoing assessments and the knowledge of all practitioners and parents/carers who have worked with the child. This evidence will have been collected in a range of ways, including:

– Photographs.
– Written observations (long and short observations).
– Video evidence.
– Audio recordings.
– Samples of recorded work.

Practitioners should link all evidence to the 'development matters' statements in the EYFS framework. Evidence to support framework must then be closely matched with the scale points of each assessment scale in the profile. These judgements should be updated regularly.

O⸺ Key Points

- Assessment in the EYFS should never be carried out by one practitioner. Effective assessment is a collaborative process and should include all practitioners in the setting, children, and their parents and carers. Lead practitioners in settings should spend time modelling effective assessment strategies to other staff in the setting, and parents or carers should be informed about how they can contribute to assessment.
- Practitioners should meet with colleagues within their own setting and between settings to develop a shared understanding of judgements in relation to the EYFS profile.

How do profile scores support children's learning and development?

Although the profile is a summative assessment of a child's attainment, to be completed at the end of the EYFS, many practitioners update each child's profile record during the year.

Practitioners are able to draw on their day-to-day assessment records and evidence (including observations, samples of children's work, photographic evidence, and audio and visual evidence, as well as evidence supplied by parents) to complete the profile each term. These day-to-day assessments are often linked to the 'development matters' statements in the EYFS framework. This enables practitioners to plan for each child's next steps in learning. However, the Early Learning Goals and the profile scale points are often interlinked so that practitioners can draw on their ongoing assessments to update the profile during the year. Practitioners are then able to identify whether children are likely to attain in line with national expectations by the end of the EYFS. This information enables practitioners to determine whether a child requires intervention or whether there are significant trends among groups of learners, such as gender or ethnicity. The information also enables practitioners to identify any weaknesses in specific areas of learning, either with specific groups or with the whole cohort.

National Foundation Stage Profile data indicates that boys achieve less well than girls across all areas of learning (DCSF 2007a). This is particularly apparent in communication, language and literacy, where inspection evidence indicates a gap between the attainment of boys and girls (Ofsted 2007). Practitioners are able to use assessment data to evaluate their practice and modify aspects of their provision. For example, if the profile data indicates that boys' attainment in writing is well below national expectations, then practitioners might consider providing more meaningful contexts and genuine purposes for writing as a way of engaging boys with this aspect of the curriculum. This reflects an action research-style approach for practitioners, and the effectiveness of the intervention can be evaluated when profile scores are next updated. If profile data indicates that specific groups of ethnic learners are achieving significantly less than other groups of learners, this should raise interesting questions for practitioners, such as

- What areas of learning are specific issues for this group of learners?

- Is the current provision inclusive for different ethnic groups? If not, could this provide an explanation for significant underachievement?

- How can the provision be enhanced to reflect the cultural experiences of this specific group?

The profile data can therefore be used to identify gaps in provision rather than for identifying children's next steps. Clearly, practitioners will need to pay careful attention to children's attainment in PSED. We argue here that although all six areas of learning are equally weighted, underachievement in PSED will inevitably impact on children's achievement across the five other areas of learning. If children do not have good dispositions for learning, lack perseverance and have low self-esteem, this will impact significantly on the rest of the curriculum. If profile data indicates that attainment in PSED is weak, practitioners will need to ensure that emphasis is placed on developing these important skills, attitudes, dispositions and characteristics. Some children may require specific intervention in PSED, and the profile data will support any initial 'gut feelings' which practitioners may hold.

We argue that the approaches described here do not in any way suggest the use of the profile as a formative tool for planning next steps for individual learners. The purpose of updating the profile during the year is to enable practitioners to identify trends among groups of learners and weaknesses in provision that, if addressed, will make a significant difference to attainment at the end of the EYFS. We also stress that the Foundation Stage profile should not be used as a deficit model to identify what children have not achieved. Hutchin (2007) stresses that assessment in the EYFS should focus on children's significant achievements. Assessment records should not focus on what children are unable to do. Assessment evidence should celebrate all children's achievements, however small they may be. Using the profile in the way suggested here enables practitioners to evaluate their provision and practice and to identify emerging trends during the year. Practitioners should plan for children's 'next steps' in learning rather than obsessively focusing on whether children are working above or below national expectations.

Reception class practitioners have to balance the principles of effective assessment in the EYFS with the top-down standards agenda and close monitoring of the attainment/outcomes in their provision by the local authority and the DCSF. Finding the balance is no easy task. The EYFS is one phase of education, with one set of principles applicable to all age groups within this phase. However, under current policy, practitioners in the final year of the Foundation Stage are heavily accountable for the outcomes their learners attain. These outcomes, which are compared to national expectations, may ultimately drive pedagogical approaches within the final year of the Foundation Stage. This is a cause for concern. It would appear that in many respects the notion of the *unique child* is diluted by the fact that judgements about the quality and effectiveness of settings are made on the basis of the proportion of learners who attain national standards across the six areas of learning. The current emphasis on children's attainment in CLL and problem solving, reasoning and numeracy

(PRSN) at the end of the Foundation Stage by inspection teams and local authorities may impact negatively on pedagogical approaches. This may undermine the principles of effective practice in the EYFS. Effective practitioners are committed to the principles of effective practice as set out in the EYFS, and provide young children with a broad range of rich, stimulating experiences to support their learning. These practitioners value all areas of learning equally and use assessment to identify what learners know and can do. Children's next steps in learning are clearly identified, and children are not categorised and labelled into groups.

Parents and the EYFSP

More extensive guidance on involving parents in assessment is included in Chapter 8. The key point is to create a climate where parents feel able to talk to practitioners and share information about their child's learning at home. The EYFSP has a formal expectation that parent and children's views will be included in the final assessment. This is the only national, compulsory summative assessment where both the voices of parents and children are included (Hutchin 2007).

The child's ongoing record of achievement ultimately informs the EYFSP. Practitioners should draw on this information to make the final judgements against the profile scale points. Therefore it makes good sense to involve parents or carers as partners in the completion of the learning journey for their child. Parental contributions are valuable, as it is important to remember that learning takes place both at home and in the setting, and the learning which takes place outside the setting should be valued, documented and discussed with parents. It is therefore beneficial for parents and practitioners to meet regularly to discuss children's learning at home and to reflect on this. Parents and practitioners can engage in reflective dialogue about the assessment evidence that has been collected from outside the setting. Working collaboratively, they can then analyse the evidence in terms of what it tells them about children's learning and development by linking the learning to the EYFS framework and the profile. Both parents and practitioners can then use the framework to identify children's next steps in learning.

This approach to assessment challenges practitioners to recognise that the child's learning at home is valuable and should be celebrated. Ofsted (2007) noted that settings often consulted with parents on their child's learning on entry to the setting but that consultation with parents becomes less frequent over time. According to Hutchin (2007: 71), 'a truly reciprocal relationship with parents goes far beyond the settling-in or transition period.' This is important, as it reminds practitioners that consultation with parents or carers should be regular and non-hierarchical. Practitioners should encourage parents to document children's learning outside the setting, and this information should be included in children's learning journeys. The views of the parents should be included in the child's profile record and practitioners should actively seek these views.

O━ Key Point

- Encourage parents to contribute to the EYFSP. Ask them to take photographs of children's holistic learning at home and include these photographs in the child's learning journey. Encourage parents to write short observations of children at home and include these in the child's learning journey.

Involving children in the EYFSP

Susan Isaacs in 1924 emphasised the need to listen to children, so the idea of listening to children and acting on their views is nothing new. Hutchin (2007) identifies key principles which should underpin practice in the EYFS. One of these principles is that *children must be involved in their own assessment and their voices heard, regardless of age or ability.* Article 12 of the United Nations Convention on the Rights of the Child (UNESCO 1989) enshrines in law children's rights to express their opinions and to have their opinions taken into account. Britain signed this agreement in 1991. Article 12 states that

> State Parties shall assure to the child who is capable of forming his or her own opinion the right to express these views freely in all matters affecting the child, the views of the child being given due weight in accordance with the age and maturity of the child.

Hutchin (2007) stresses the importance of hearing what children say as opposed to simply listening to them. She argues that the implications of this are for practitioners to *respond* and *take action.* This is an important point with implications for practitioners. Children should be consulted about their interests and needs, and practitioners should ensure that these are taken into account in planning, teaching and provision within the setting.

Hutchin (2007) is keen to emphasise that practitioners should share observations and assessments with the child and allow children free access to their assessment record. She also stresses that children should be allowed to select some of their own sources of evidence to add to the record, thus making the process truly collaborative. Practitioners should try to find dedicated blocks of time when they can sit down with individual children to discuss the assessment evidence within the learning journey. Children need to be able to articulate their own progress, and sharing the record with the child in this way will facilitate this. In addition, children should be given frequent opportunities to share their assessment records with other children in the setting.

The Coram Family's 'Listening to Young Children' project (Clark and Moss 2001) was based on the principle that children are experts in their own learning. The project focused on a range of ways in which practitioners can actively listen to children. They referred to this as the *mosaic approach.* According to Miller et al. (2005: 55):

> Talking with children about what they have drawn can reveal a lot: how they feel about themselves, their families, friends, their environment, or, indeed, you. Giving children cameras and asking them to take photographs provides another snapshot of what they consider important. This 'mosaic' of ways of listening helps children to express themselves, thereby bringing to light any problems they may be experiencing and giving practitioners a deeper understanding of their personal, social and emotional development.

The different pieces of evidence can fit together like the pieces in a mosaic. Malaguzzi, the founder of the Reggio Emilia approach, discusses the hundred languages that children are born with. According to Malaguzzi (1993), by the age of 6, children have lost 98 of these languages. Practitioners should therefore empower children to use all modes of representation, including drawing, painting, mark-making, dance, drama, facial gestures, etc. Within the mosaic approach, the children document their learning in a wide range of ways and then practitioners and children together reflect on the learning that has taken place. This enables the practitioner to collect the child's perspectives on this learning. A significant issue for practitioners is the challenge of how to collect the voices of children who do not speak English and those with additional needs, such as children with language delay. These children have been traditionally excluded from expressing their voice, but the *Every Child Matters* agenda emphasises the need for all children to participate and have a voice. Wood and Attfield (2005) argue that this freedom of different modes of representation is valuable for children with additional needs, especially those children who may have difficulties with language and communication.

Hutchin (2007) stresses that children need to be provided with the opportunity to reflect back on their development. In the EYFSP, practitioners are required to document a conversation with a child about their learning. However, effective practitioners consult with children much more frequently. Involving children *in* the assessment process is substantially different from traditional practices where assessment was carried out *on* the child. It places children at the centre of the assessment process and provides them with a genuine opportunity to shape the process. In this approach no assessment evidence is secret or confidential, as was often the case in traditional approaches to assessment. Children, parents, carers and all practitioners in the setting should have unlimited access to the records of children's achievements. Children should be provided with opportunities to select the evidence for inclusion in the assessment record, and the learning journey should facilitate a dialogue between practitioners and children, children and parents, and children and their peers.

Practitioners need to plan opportunities to have regular conversations with children about their learning, likes and dislikes, and strengths and areas for development. Hutchin (2007) advises that questions need to be carefully framed. Additionally, children need time to think about questions before responding, and it is important not to overload children with questions (Gura and Hall 2000). Hutchin (2007) believes that it may be ineffective to interview children in a group, as this could result in children providing similar responses. Individual conferences with children may therefore be the best approach. The role of the practitioner is to listen to what children say and take a genuine interest. The practitioner will need to take notes or might digitally record the conversation. Hutchin (2007) suggests a range of questions that practitioners might consider using in these conferences. These are presented below:

- What do you like doing best at home/in the setting?

- What do you think you can do now that you couldn't do when you were younger?

- What do you think you learn in the setting?

- What do you think you learn at home?

- What do you think you are really good at doing?

- What do you find it hard to do? What don't you like doing?

- What is your favourite toy/book/game/DVD/song?
  (adapted from Hutchin 2007)

Practitioners may initially find that children's answers are brief. Therefore practitioners might wish to consider modelling some answers by talking to children about what they enjoy learning and find difficult. These conversations can be written up and included in the child's learning journey.

Key Point

- Collect the views of children in relation to their learning and incorporate these into children's learning journey and their profile record. Allow children free access to their learning journey and spend time discussing the evidence with each child.

Analysis of profile data

This chapter has suggested that analysis of profile data should not be a task undertaken solely at the end of the year. If practitioners are regularly updating the profile (at least once a term), they can start the process of analysis much earlier in the year, and this is likely to have a significant impact on overall attainment at the end of the EYFS. If practitioners are able to spot trends of under-achievement across areas of learning and across groups of learners, this can aid the process of reflection and modification of pedagogical approaches.

Likewise, practitioners also need to analyse their data at the end of the year. The following are key questions that the practitioner needs to ask when looking at the overall profile data:

- Group trends: *Are any* groups of learners *underachieving and, if so, in which areas of learning is this underachievement evident?* Data will need to be analysed by gender, ethnicity and age. For example, are there any differences in attainment between September entrants and January entrants to the EYFS?

- Cohort trends: *Does underachievement exist in specific areas of learning across a cohort? If so, can this be explained?*

- Coherence between areas of learning: *Does the data indicate evidence of parity of scores between areas of learning?* For example, if a child has a high score in PSED, are scores also consistently high across the other areas of learning? Does a low score in PSED result in low scores in other areas of learning? What is the relationship between scores in language for communication and thinking and reading and writing?

- Year-on-year trends: Practitioners should compare the data to data from the previous years. *Are there any patterns or trends evident?* Consistently low attainment in a specific area of learning will indicate the need for action planning and intervention. Part of this intervention could be support from the local authority.

- What are the strengths of the provision?

- What are the weaknesses of the provision?

- What are the issues that the Year 1 practitioner needs to focus on? It would be useful to involve the Year 1 practitioner in the analysis of the EYFSP data.

Some local authorities may carry out this analysis for Foundation Stage practitioners. The local authority will scrutinise the data and ask the lead practitioner key questions. It is important for practitioners to be able to explain any anomalies in the data or any dips or increases in attainment. The data and resulting analysis will form the basis of the self-evaluation form. The *self-evaluation* should inform and feed into the *action plan*, which will identify key priorities for immediate action. A longer-term *development plan* should be drawn up. This will detail the priorities and actions to be implemented over a period of 3 years to improve the quality of the provision. Parents and children should be consulted on the development plan, as well as all practitioners in the setting.

Case Study: Beth: Reception class

Read the following case study and think carefully about the links between PSED and other areas of learning.

Beth, a practitioner in a Reception class, was asked for profile data in April 2008. She submitted the required data in good faith. Beth was experienced in assessing children's learning and was very aware that *attainment* overall in her school was low. In relation to national expectations, attainment on entry to Reception was low overall, but value-added data indicated that children had made outstanding *progress* by the end of the Foundation Stage. Beth was aware that despite very good value-added scores, data at the end of the Foundation Stage was not generally in line with national expectations.

Over a period of several years Beth had noted that on entry to the final year of the EYFS, learners' attainment across all aspects of PSED had been significantly low. Beth felt strongly that attainment in PSED underpinned attainment in all other areas of learning. PSED therefore became a focus in this setting. Beth had found that once learners had begun to make good progress in all aspects of PSED, progress in other areas gradually increased. The key to progress across all areas of learning hinged on attainment in PSED being an initial priority, despite the fact that all six areas of learning have an equal weighting.

The local authority analysed the data submitted by this setting in April 2008. The analysis raised questions for further consideration by Beth. Beth valued this analysis; however, she had concerns relating to the links made between attainment in all aspects of PSED and CLL. Perceived anomalies between PSED and CLL scores were highlighted in the data. The local authority questioned the validity of any scores that indicated higher attainment in PSED than in CLL. In reality, Beth had found that a focus on learners' attainment in PSED had impacted positively on all the other five areas of learning. However, the link between PSED and CLL was problematic for Beth, due to the fact that attainment in the two areas of learning did not move in tandem. Children with strong scores in PSED were better equipped to address learning across the four aspects of CLL. However, Beth had observed that children's progress in CLL only started to show marked improvement *after* children had reached a good level of attainment in PSED. It was therefore logical to Beth that attainment in CLL lagged behind attainment in PSED.

It was apparent that by the end of June 2008 practitioners would be required to report to the local authority the percentage of

(Continued)

children in any one cohort who had achieved national expectations across all aspects of PSED and CLL. Many of the children in this cohort had achieved national expectations in all aspects of PSED, but not in all aspects of CLL. Despite this, value-added data in CLL was strong. Data collection systems, in June 2008, showed that 0 per cent of this cohort had achieved scores demonstrating achievement at national expectations in relation to CLL. The practitioner found this cold data collection, and the interpretation of the data, frustrating. Despite clearly identifying the specific needs of the children in the setting, she felt that, on paper, her practice was seen as ineffective.

- Why was Beth frustrated?
- Do you think there is a positive correlation between children's scores in PSED and other areas of learning?
- How might attainment in linking sounds and letters impact on children's attainment in reading and writing?
- How might attainment in language for communication and thinking impact on attainment in other areas?

⩔ Reflective Activity

Look at the Table in Figure 7.1. The table shows Foundation Stage exit profile scores for a class of children.

- Which children require specific intervention in specific areas to raise their levels of attainment?
- Work out the percentage of children who have reached national expectations in each area of learning (take national expectations to mean 6 scale points).
- Which areas of learning are strong and which are weak?
- Which children have inconsistent scores across specific areas of learning? How might this be explained?
- Which children are working above national expectations in specific areas of learning? How might these children be challenged further in Year 1?

⊶ Key Points

- Consider carefully the information your profile data can provide. This should be an ongoing process through the final year of the EYFS. Some prompts to aid this are included below:

- Is there a difference between the attainment of boys and girls? If so, which aspects of learning does this apply to?
- What is the impact of starting the Reception class after the autumn term?
- Are there any global trends relating to attainment?
- Are there any trends relating to the attainment of different ethnic groups?
- What is the impact of one child on overall attainment? In a small cohort, one child can carry a high percentage. Be prepared to justify your data in view of this.

• If you can identify any emerging issues throughout the year in terms of children's attainment, appropriate intervention at an early stage might help to secure high standards by the end of the year. Specific interventions will vary from targeting individual children or groups of children to modifying classroom provision and pedagogical approaches for groups and individuals.

	DA	SD	ED	LCT	LSL	Read	Wri	NLC	Calc	SSM	KUW	PD	CD	Total
Callum (M)	5	5	4	4	3	3	3	2	2	3	3	4	4	45
Jasmine (F)	8	6	7	7	7	7	6	4	4	4	6	7	7	80
Frances (F)	7	6	7	7	5	6	5	4	5	5	4	7	6	74
Fred (M)	8	6	7	7	7	7	7	7	7	7	6	4	7	87
Chris (M)	8	6	7	7	7	7	6	7	6	7	5	7	7	87
Sophie (F)	8	6	7	7	7	7	6	7	5	6	5	7	6	84
Rashad (M)	7	6	5	7	7	7	6	7	7	7	6	7	5	84
Hang (F)	6	6	4	4	4	3	1	4	3	3	3	6	5	52
Jack (M)	7	5	4	3	3	3	3	2	2	3	2	5	4	46
Angel (F)	8	6	6	7	6	5	6	6	5	6	5	7	7	80
Paul (M)	8	6	7	7	7	6	6	7	6	6	6	7	7	86
Abdul (M)	7	6	7	7	5	6	5	4	5	5	4	7	6	74
Joseph (M)	5	6	6	6	6	5	5	5	5	5	4	7	6	71
James (M)	6	5	4	4	3	4	4	6	5	3	3	7	4	58
Stephanie (F)	6	5	4	4	3	4	4	4	4	4	4	6	4	56
Selina (F)	7	6	5	6	5	5	5	7	6	6	6	6	7	77
Chiku (F)	4	4	6	5	3	3	1	6	3	3	3	5	3	49
Kayleigh (F)	8	6	7	7	6	6	6	7	7	7	6	7	8	88
Carl (M)	5	5	5	5	3	4	3	4	3	3	3	6	4	53
John (M)	8	6	5	6	7	6	5	7	6	5	4	7	6	78
Fuji (F)	8	5	6	7	5	5	5	7	6	6	6	7	6	79
Hannah (F)	6	5	4	3	3	4	3	1	2	2	2	6	3	44
Oliver (M)	5	5	5	5	4	4	3	6	5	3	4	5	4	58
Patrick (M)	8	6	5	7	7	7	7	7	7	7	6	7	7	88
ChingLan (F)	5	5	6	6	6	5	4	6	6	6	6	5	5	71

Figure 7.1 Foundation Stage profile exit scores

New possibilities

This chapter acknowledges that the EYFSP is a summative assessment tool. Its prime purpose is to summarise children's learning at the end of the Foundation Stage. However, we have suggested that the profile can be used in a formative way during the final year of the Foundation Stage by identifying broad targets early which children need to achieve. Practitioners should use the EYFS framework to plan children's next steps in learning, but broader targets for individuals and groups of learners can be identified from the profile.

Further Reading

National Assessment Agency (2008) *Quality Assurance of Early Years Foundation Stage Profile Data*. NAA.

- This guidance document is excellent because it provides practitioners with an overview of effective quality assurance procedures and guidance on the use and analysis of profile data. It provides practitioners with possible lines of enquiry for interrogation of profile data.

Useful Website

www.lancsngfl.ac.uk/curriculum/assessment/index.php?category_id=2

- This website is excellent because it includes portfolios of assessment evidence with judgements about children's learning. There is also guidance on this site for ways of using the EYFSP in Year 1.

8

Involving parents and carers as partners in assessment

Jonathan Glazzard

Chapter Objectives

- To explore the contribution that parents/carers can make to formative and summative assessment across the six areas of learning in the Early Years Foundation Stage (EYFS).
- To support trainee practitioners in identifying the importance of actively engaging parents in understanding individual learner's attainment and their next steps in learning.
- To draw on examples of good practice from a range of settings.

This chapter explores the role of parents/carers as partners in assessment of children's learning and development within the Early Years Foundation Stage (EYFS). The chapter draws on examples of case studies from settings that support effective practice. New trainee practitioners frequently find the assessment requirements of the EYFS both daunting and complex. This chapter will explore and unpick the key issues relating to parents/carers as partners in assessment.

Parents, carers and practitioners as an assessment team

In *The Early Years Foundation Stage*, the DCSF (2008c) states:

> Parents are children's first and most enduring educators. When parents and practitioners work together in early years settings, the results have a positive impact on children's development and learning. (DCFS 2008c: 2.2)

Hutchin (2007) believes that involving the parents in assessments needs to begin before a child enters a setting. Thus, the home visit provides a rich context for collecting data on children's learning and development. Parents can help practitioners to identify a baseline assessment through initial discussion, samples of recorded work completed at home, and photographs of the child engaged in a wide range of activities. The evidence collected can then be included in the child's learning journey.

 Case Study: Developing a working party: Reception class

Read the following case study and think carefully about how value systems shape the practice.

This case study relates to a setting in a socially deprived area. This setting identified a need to engage parents and carers in the assessment process. Practitioners in the setting value parents and carers as equal partners in assessment of children's learning and development. The staff invited a group of parents and carers to form a working party. The purpose of the working party was to develop a policy in partnership with parents and carers. Additionally, the policy had to reflect individual learning and development both at home and at school. To ensure that the policy was effective in practice, it was essential that it was manageable and achievable for busy parents and carers. As a result of the working party, it quickly became evident that the confidence and understanding of those involved grew rapidly. All members of the group were willing and enthusiastic.

Systems to record individual learning and development were already established in this setting. Individual learning journeys relating to the six areas of the EYFS framework were openly available to parents and carers. At this point these records had been the responsibility of practitioners within the setting. The learning journeys included a range of evidence to support judgements relating to individual attainment and next steps. The local authority considered these to be effective working documents. These learning journeys became a model for supporting parents and carers in building on evidence of their own child's individual learning and development. Previously, parents and carers had been given regular opportunities to view and discuss individual learning journeys with the practitioner in the setting. They had been well informed of current attainment and identified individual next steps in all six areas of learning. However, parents and carers clearly saw assessment and learning as the sole responsibility of practitioners.

The working party had considered ways in which parents and carers could effectively manage and contribute to enhancing the learning journeys. Supported by the working party, the lead practitioner invited parents and carers to a launch event. The purpose of this event was to develop parents' and carers' understanding of children as learners both at home and at school. It was important to acknowledge that both home and school provide a wide range of opportunities for learning and that children may behave very differently at home from the way they behave in school. Learning and development in both contexts needed to be acknowledged and evidenced. Ways of evidencing achievements within home contexts were shared with parents at the initial meeting. The learning journeys were shared with parents and carers, and the range of evidence included within them was discussed. Parents and carers were invited to make their own contributions to these learning journeys through the use of observations, recorded work and photographs in the home context.

Members of the working party now had a clear understanding of the EYFS framework and effective assessment measured against it. The working party became a valuable point of contact for other parents and carers. Parents and carers were initially reluctant to contribute directly to the learning journeys. They lacked the confidence to do so. The working party acknowledged this and devised a means of facilitating parental contributions to assessment. A 'Wow Wall' was developed. This enabled parents to celebrate their child's achievements at home. They readily brought work, photographs and some observations into the setting and shared these with practitioners. Staff in the setting valued all contributions, and parents and carers were equally invited to celebrate their child's successes by completing a 'Wow' certificate and displaying it alongside evidence of their child's achievements on the Wow Wall. Practitioners discussed these assessments with the parents/carers. Parents and carers seemed to lack the confidence to link their assessments with the EYFS framework, but this problem was easily

(Continued)

addressed by practitioners in the setting taking on this important role. Parents, carers and practitioners were now all effective contributors to this assessment evidence. At a later date the practitioners transferred this evidence to the learning journeys.

- What values were evident in this case study?
- How do these values help to create an inclusive ethos?
- Do all members of staff in your setting subscribe to a set of shared values for working in partnership with parents and carers?
- Are there any members of staff with conflicting values? How might staff work together to form a set of shared values?

Key Points

- Invite parents and carers to contribute to the policies of the setting. You may consider developing a working party consisting of parents, carers and practitioners. The working party can discuss new initiatives and contribute ideas to support the development of effective practice and policies within the setting.
- It is important to evaluate the impact of new initiatives. Evaluation should take account of the views of a range of stakeholders, including parents, carers, staff and children.

Valuing parents' and carers' contributions to formative assessment

Parents may bring assessment evidence into the setting in a range of formats. This could be:

- Photographs of the child.

- Samples of 'work'.

- Models the child has made.

Value these forms of evidence and talk to the parent about what information these sources give you. Start to include them in the child's learning journey. Over time, gradually ask the parents to extend the range of evidence. Ask them to produce jottings or notes based on observations. Ask them to tape-record their child's conversations. Ask them to video evidence of significant achievement. This could be very easily done by using a mobile phone and the evidence could be emailed to you. Incorporate this evidence in the child's learning journey. Essentially, if you demonstrate that you value the evidence, over a period of time the parents should start to extend the range of evidence they provide you with. Emphasise that you are interested in evidence of achievement. You are interested in what the child can do. The focus must be on the positive aspects of learning.

Communicating attainment and next steps to parents and carers

Parents and carers need to be informed about children's next steps in learning. It is considered to be good practice to work together with parents to formulate the next steps. Parents will often have their own thoughts about what they want their child to be able to do next. You might find it useful to refer to the milestones in the EYFS framework and use these to plan the next steps in conjunction with parents and carers. Parents will be able to do this confidently themselves if they are provided with a copy of the EYFS framework. However, emphasise that the starting point must be where the child is. Stress that children are unique learners and they progress at different rates. It is also important to stress that children's attainment may not be consistent across all six areas of learning.

🔑 Key Points

- Create regular opportunities for parents and carers to discuss their child's achievements. Together identify ways in which you can support progression and jointly identify the next steps.
- Ensure that parents understand the next steps in all six areas of learning and encourage them to support their child in working towards these steps.

Enabling parents and carers to become confident assessors

It might be useful to share examples of practitioner observations and annotated photographs with parents before asking them to complete assessments themselves at home. Parents can therefore benefit from models of good practice. You could invite parents into the setting to observe practitioners observing young children's learning. You could then follow the observation with a debrief session. Parents and practitioners can discuss what they have both observed, and then the evidence can be matched to the EYFS goals. In this respect, practitioners can act as mentors to parents. You could invite parents to informal training sessions where you train them in observational techniques. The key point is that in order to *enable* parents to become assessors, you will need to give them the confidence that they can do it, and they need to know that their observations are valuable and necessary.

The REPEY research (Siraj-Blatchford et al. 2002) acknowledges that staff may need to be more proactive in influencing and supporting a home learning environment, and some parents may be reluctant to engage with education or assessment of learning at home. Some parents will have formed assumptions about the role of home and school and created an artificial dividing line between the two. These parents will be more of a challenge in terms of developing effective partnerships. In these circumstances, it will be necessary to work harder at developing interactions and discussions with these parents. Take every opportunity to talk to parents informally and strike up a relationship. Ultimately, you will need to convince these parents why their knowledge of the child in the home environment should be shared with you. Once relationships are established and secure, you will then be able to develop partnerships focusing on learning and assessment.

Parental contributions to the EYFSP

The guidance for the EYFSP states:

> Assessment must actively engage parents and/or other primary carers, the first educators of children, or it will offer an incomplete picture. Accurate assessment requires a two-way flow of information between setting(s) and home and reviews of the child's achievements should include those demonstrated at home. (QCA 2008: 10)

The profile is a summative assessment of a child's achievements at the end of the Foundation Stage and parents should be equal partners in its completion. However, it has been found by Ofsted (2007) that parental involvement in the summative judgements at the end of the Foundation Stage is not common. Involving parents in assessment is a challenge to practitioners. It challenges traditional assumptions about the role of the practitioner as the one with responsibility to make judgements about children's learning and development. It challenges the traditional power divide between parents and professionals. It raises questions about the value of professionalism and the distinction between parent and teacher/practitioner. These debates, although very interesting, must be put aside. Research evidence (Siraj-Blatchford et al. 2002) suggests that outcomes for children are the highest where information is shared between parents and staff and where staff involve parents in decision making. Practitioners need to embrace new and exciting models of learning. Ofsted (2007) note that true partnerships with parents are rare, but where partnerships do exist, there is a significant impact on achievement. Practitioners need to reflect on their own values before engaging with parents in partnership. In particular, practitioners need to consider:

- Whether they consider themselves more knowledgeable about children as learners than parents.

- Whether they truly value parental contributions to the assessment process or whether they think their own assessments are more important.

- Whether they consider parents to be equal partners in their child's education.

- Whether their policies on parent partnership are truly inclusive and engage all parents.

Once these questions have been considered, practitioners need to plan carefully the approaches they intend to use to engage parents in the assessment process. It is not possible to do everything at once. The partnership will need to evolve and be flexible. Practitioners might consider developing a working group, consisting of staff, parents and children. This group might be responsible for policy development within the setting. Parent partnership needs to permeate every aspect of the setting, and parents will need training in the principles of effective early years practice if they are to understand the complexities of assessment in the Foundation Stage.

Judgements made for the EYFSP provide a summary of each child's achievements at the end of the Foundation Stage. These judgements can then be compared with national expectations of children's attainment. A summary of a child's attainment at the end of the Foundation stage is incomplete if practitioners fail to engage parents and carers in the process of assessment. Children learn both at home and in settings, and judgements about learning need to take into account the learning which has taken place in both settings. Parents and carers have a deep knowledge of what their children know and can do. Effective practitioners value this knowledge and actively seek parents' views on children's learning.

According to the National Assessment Agency (NAA) (2008),

> Children have many different experiences outside of the school setting and these must be taken into consideration when completing the EYFS profile. (NAA 2008: 2)

Practitioners can learn a great deal about children's learning and development from parents and vice versa. Involving parents as partners in assessment will ultimately help parents to understand more about learning and development, and parents can begin to understand the role of play as a facilitator of learning. In genuine partnerships, settings should involve parents in writing policies and enlist their support in shaping the future direction of the setting. Parents can therefore be involved in developing policy and practice in terms of assessment.

The starting point for practitioners is to establish meaningful relationships with parents and carers. If parents and carers do not feel confident in sharing information with the practitioner, it is likely that they will be unwilling to be active partners in the assessment process. It is therefore vital that all practitioners respect parents and value what they have to say. You need to spend time talking to the parents and listening to what they have to say about their children. Try to be friendly at all times and take their concerns seriously. It is important to demonstrate to parents that their views are listened to and valued.

∿ Reflective Activity

Read the following scenario from a setting in a deprived community.

A setting has recently introduced an initiative to support parents/carers as partners in assessments. The practitioners have invited parents to an introductory meeting and newsletters have been distributed. The aim of the initiative is to invite parents to contribute to their

child's learning journey by including parental observations completed at home. Millie is a very withdrawn child, and her mother
acknowledges that this is typical behaviour for Millie until she feels
safe and secure with adults and peers. She supports this by saying:

> You ought to see her with her granddad. She is full of it.

The practitioner is interested in pursuing this statement and invites
Millie's mum to contribute a short observation relating to Millie's
interaction with her granddad. Her response to this is:

> Why me? That is your job. I'm her mum, not a teacher!

- Consider how you would respond and encourage Millie's mum
  to become a partner in the assessment process?
- How would you persuade Millie's mum that her contributions to
  the assessment process are vital?

Celebrating achievements at home

Finding time to meet with parents is never an easy task. Perhaps
you could ask the parents to spend some time in the setting each
morning. Encourage them to bring in photographs which evidence
significant achievement at home and ask them to write short commentaries to accompany the photograph. This evidence can then be
included in each child's personal learning journey. Try to spend
some time talking to parents about their child's learning at home.
You could ask them to write up some short observations that evidence
significant achievement. However, you may need to run a session
with them first on observational assessment. You might want to provide certificates that parents can freely access if they want to issue a
reward for significant achievement. These could be displayed on a
noticeboard and later included in the child's learning journey.
However, it is important that parents understand the effects of over-
using praise and the dangers of extrinsic motivation. In one setting
recently visited, parents had been asked to complete Post-it notes to
document evidence of their child's significant achievements at
home. These were then displayed and used as a focus for generating
a discussion with children about their learning at home.

The key point to stress is that practitioners should actively seek the
contributions of parents and carers in the assessment process. Some parents will be more reluctant to contribute than others. The practitioner
has an important role to play in encouraging parents and carers to be

partners in the assessment process. Parents need to understand why their views and contributions are important and they need to recognise the importance of the learning which takes place in the home context. Equally, as a practitioner, you need to value this learning as much as the learning which takes place in the setting.

The key challenge for practitioners is that partnership in assessment means that parental judgements should not be marginalised in favour of judgements made by practitioners. If a discrepancy arises, it is important for practitioners to discuss this openly. Children may demonstrate achievement at home that they do not demonstrate in the context of the setting, and this will need further exploration and investigation. In inclusive settings, both parents and practitioners have an equal voice and active dialogue is essential in cases where achievement may be demonstrated outside the setting but has not been witnessed in the setting. Practitioners need to provide space and time to share assessments, and children's next steps should be jointly planned and discussed together.

 Reflective Activity

Read the following scenario that highlights a significant issue where parents and practitioners seem unable to agree on judgements about Billy's learning.

Billy can be a highly motivated and inquisitive child. He asks questions, loves to investigate the world around him, and contributes effectively to discussions. Unfortunately, these attributes are inconsistent. On many occasions Billy is tired and unable to focus. The practitioners have communicated their concerns to his parents. The parents claim that Billy does not demonstrate these dispositions and attitudes at home and provide many examples of Billy's outstanding achievements at home. The practitioners have also approached parents to communicate Billy's next steps and suggest ways in which the parents might support these at home. However, the parents consistently claim that Billy is able to demonstrate these targets at home.

- How would you address the mismatch between the practitioners' judgements of Billy's attainments and the judgements made by his parents?
- How could you develop a more effective partnership with Billy's parents?
- How could you then capitalise on this partnership so that Billy's parents are willing to contribute accurately to the assessment process?

The National Assessment Agency (NAA) (2008) stresses that parental partnership in assessment is critical for families which frequently change location – for example, Gypsy, Roma or Traveller children or children who have parents in the forces. In these circumstances, parents' extensive knowledge of their children's development will be extremely useful. Practitioners can use this knowledge and their own observations to gain a full picture of the child's development. Parental partnership is also critical in the case of children with English as an additional language. For these children, all scale points except scale points 4–9 on the four communication, language and literacy scales can be achieved in a child's home language (NAA 2008). Therefore parent partnership is essential so that parents can inform the practitioner about their child's progress towards the first three scale points.

⚬━ Key Point

- Ensure that you are visible and available at specific times in the day to meet with parents and carers informally. Parents are often happy to mention the significant achievements of their children at home. Take time to talk to parents and carers and be friendly with them. Respect their valuable contributions to the assessment process. Make notes of any verbal communications with parents and carers about children's achievements and date the record.

Practical strategies for facilitating parent partnership

Some strategies to facilitate effective parent partnership in assessment are documented below.

Training

Assessment is a complex process, particularly in the early years. Children's play and child-initiated interactions form a rich source of evidence of children's learning and development. Parents and carers will benefit from some training sessions which focus on the principles of assessment in the early years, and methods of evidencing significant achievement and linking assessment to the statutory EYFS framework. Parents and carers may also benefit from some training in the EYFSP. Initially, you may be happy to accept the evidence from parents without any links to developmental milestones or profile scale points. However, as the parents become more confident, you might wish to consider offering some training on making accurate judgements on learning and development by encouraging them to make reference to the milestones in the EYFS framework. Parents will then be able to identify their child's next steps more accurately. You can then invite parents to termly meetings where day-to-day assessments are considered against the EYFSP.

Home visits

Home visits before children join the setting provide a rich context for assessment. Spend some time talking to parents about the child's interests, dispositions and attitudes. Document this discussion, date it and add it to the child's learning journey. Try to take photographs of the child in the home environment and add these to the child's journal. Talk to the parents about the importance of play as a vehicle for learning and explain to parents the role of adult interaction in play. If parents understand what children are learning through play, they are more likely to be able to identify significant learning and achievement in the home context. This will be useful when you start to involve parents in observational assessments of their child in the home context.

Key Point

- Visit the children at home to find out about their individual interests and use these visits to develop positive professional relationships with their parents or carers. Take photographs of children's play and interests at home after seeking parental permission. Include these in the child's learning journey. Incorporate children's individual interests at home into your planning. Children who are interested and motivated will achieve higher outcomes.

Learning diaries, learning journeys and learning stories

Some setting use home–school diaries to document evidence of a child's learning during the day. Practitioners may include photographs, observations of learning or quotes from conversations they may have had with the child. These can then be sent home to form a focus for discussion between the parent and the child. Parents can then add their own assessment evidence to the learning diary as a way of informing the practitioner about children's learning in the home context. Carr (2001) discusses the value of 'learning stories' and parental involvement with these. These stories document the learning which has taken place during the day. They can be shared with the parents, who can enjoy reading rich accounts about their child's daily experiences. The stories are a document of the child's holistic development and they can provide a catalyst for discussion between the child and the parent/carer. Learning stories are a valuable vehicle through which children can revisit learning which has taken place during the day. In settings with limited numbers of staff, learning stories are more difficult to manage, and in these situations staff may wish to document the child's significant achievements over time in a learning journey. This can be freely available in the setting for parents to refer to. However, it can also be sent home periodically and shared with the parents.

Key Points

- Ensure that children's learning journeys are a shared document that parents can access at any time. Ensure that there is a suitable place for parents to read these documents. Encourage parents to bring photographs into the setting which provide evidence of their child's learning at home. Also encourage parents to bring in samples of individual achievements at home, including recorded outcomes or notes which parents have made on the basis of observations. Value all of these contributions to the assessment process and include this evidence in the child's learning journey.
- Learning journeys are a positive document and record a child's achievements. Invite parents and carers into the setting to share these learning journeys with their child on a regular basis.

 Case Study: Home–school diaries: Reception class

Read the following case study, which focuses on the introduction of home–school diaries.

In the same setting as described in the previous case study, there were further developments to inform parents of achievements and

(Continued)

next steps in learning on a more regular basis as an ongoing process. The introduction of the Wow Wall had had a very positive impact on parental contributions to the assessment process. It was notable that many more parents were approaching the practitioners to share their child's successes and they were enthusiastic about ensuring that their child's achievements at home were included on the Wow Wall. Dialogue between home and school was clearly enhanced.

As the interest and enthusiasm of the parents and carers grew, the practitioners identified a need to communicate much more frequently with parents and carers about their children's achievements and next steps in all six areas of learning. The practitioners had considered the introduction of home–school diaries, and this initiative was introduced to the working party for further consideration.

It was agreed that the home–school diaries would be trialled. Parents and carers were informed about the initiative through a newsletter. The diaries facilitated effective communication, on a daily basis, between home and school. Parents, carers and practitioners alike commented on children's achievements and difficulties. This enabled practitioners to identify next steps. The practitioners were also able to advise parents and carers of exciting, practical ways in which they could support their child's learning and next steps.

During this process, data was collected in relation to this initiative. The data showed that 80 per cent of parents and carers were contributing to the diaries at least three times a week. The practitioners were fully aware that 20 per cent of parents/carers were not contributing to the daily diaries. In an effort to address this, a visible parent information board was devised to inform parents and carers about the learning taking place in the setting each week. Parents were also consulted about their views on the effectiveness of the diaries. An overwhelming majority declared that they were useful and that they wished this new initiative to continue. From the beginning the practitioners were aware that it was important to avoid overloading the parents with information. Comments in the diaries focused on significant individual achievement, next steps in learning and misconceptions that the children were experiencing.

The practitioners valued the comments made by parents and carers in the diaries. Both these comments and observational assessments in the setting contributed to accurate judgements relating to individual attainment. Parental comments were included in the children's learning journeys.

- What strategies might you put into place to encourage all parents to contribute to the home–school diaries?
- How might you address situations where parents or carers directly challenge your comments in the home–school diary?
- What sort of information might you or your colleagues include in a home–school diary? What aspects of learning might you focus on?

Achievement wall

This wall can be a celebration of a child's achievements, either in the home setting or in the context of the setting. Parents and practitioners can contribute to this jointly. You can encourage parents to add photographs and captions to the wall, or you might want to use special praise certificates or slips. These can be added to the child's learning journal at a later date.

Verbal evidence

Conversations with parents and carers provide rich sources of evidence for assessment. You will need to document and date the conversation, and this evidence can then be included in the child's learning journey. Conversations with parents can often be useful in terms of enabling practitioners to formulate a more holistic view of a child's achievements. For example, a child may be reluctant to initiate interactions in the setting but may demonstrate more confidence in the home. Remember to find the time and space to collect as much information from the parents as you can. The context of the activity needs to be clearly documented to make moderation easier.

Making learning visible

The NAA (2008) recommends that assessments of children's learning should be made visible to parents. This can be done in a variety of ways such as displaying photographs of children's learning on a wall and using the interactive whiteboard to display photographs of children's learning. This is particularly effective if the photographic images are played in a loop so that a cycle of images is repeated. This provides a powerful vehicle for discussion with parents about children's learning.

> **O═ Key Point**
>
> - Through the use of ICT, introduce a loop of DVD footage showing children engaged in a range of activities. This should be supported by an additional commentary relating to achievements measured against the EYFS framework.

Moderation of parental assessments

There is a need to moderate assessment judgements and this is also the case for parental assessments. Therefore, you should include parental assessments in moderation events both within the setting and in cross-setting moderation. You might also want to consider involving parents in the moderation process.

The importance of values

Effective practitioners value parental contributions to assessment. They actively seek their involvement in the assessment process and empower them to contribute. These practitioners believe that parents are skilled and able to contribute equally to the assessment process. They form effective relationships with significant carers and thus help to break down barriers. Additionally, these practitioners believe that the child is a holistic learner and that learning takes place both within the setting and in the home. As a practitioner, it is important that you reflect on your own values. Do you believe that parents and carers can make valuable contributions to the assessment process, or do you place more emphasis on learning within the setting and do you value practitioner judgements over the judgements made by those closest to the child? This chapter challenges traditional notions of assessment and opens up new possibilities for practitioners to work in partnership with families and children.

Further Reading

Hutchin, V. (2007) *Supporting Every Child's Learning Across the Early Years Foundation Stage*. London: Hodder Education.

- Chapter 5 in this text has some excellent guidance about involving parents and children in assessment.

Ofsted (2007), *The Foundation Stage: A Report of 144 Settings,* HMI 2610, available on www.ofsted.gov.uk

- This document provides examples of outstanding and weak practice. It is a useful document for practitioners to benchmark the quality of their settings against.

Qualifications and Curriculum Authority, (2008) *Early years Foundation Stage Profile Handbook,* QCA.

- The profile handbook gives some useful advice on working with parents of children with English as an Additional Language.

Useful Website

www.naa.org.uk/eyfsp

- The National Assessment Agency website contains useful case study material on incorporating information from parents (December 2007).

9

What impacts on children's learning and development?

Jonathan Glazzard

Chapter Objectives

- To develop a clear understanding of inclusion.
- To know some identifying characteristics of specific special needs and strategies to support these children.
- To be aware of the implications of *Every Child Matters*.

This chapter introduces students to definitions of inclusion and the issues associated with labelling. In addition the chapter provides a brief overview of specific special needs and the characteristics of each. We emphasise here that the characteristics should not be used as a checklist for practitioners to diagnose specific special needs. Only trained and qualified professionals can officially diagnose specific needs. The chapter then includes some useful strategies for facilitating the effective inclusion of these children.

Developing inclusive practices

According to Booth et al.,

Inclusion is not another name for special educational needs ... inclusion is seen to involve the identification and minimising of barriers to learning and partici-pation and the maximising of resources to support learning and participation. (Booth et al. 2000: 13)

These authors are right to emphasise the fact that inclusion is about a deep concern for the education of all pupils, not just pupils with special educational needs. Therefore effective practitioners should consider the impact of a range of factors on learning and development. For example, practitioners need to observe carefully how gender can impact on learning, and observational assessments can be used to analyse how boys and girls are accessing different areas of provision. This information can then be used to aid evaluation of provision and areas can be changed to appeal to both boys and girls. If learning environments do not engage all learners, this can quickly become a barrier to participation and learning. As a practitioner, you should be aware of the relationship between social deprivation and underachievement and the underachievement of specific groups of learners. The Joseph Rowntree Foundation website includes a vast range of research articles on factors such as these that influence learning and development.

According to Corbett and Slee,

> Inclusive education is an unabashed announcement, a public and political declaration and celebration of difference. It requires continual proactive responsiveness to foster an inclusive education culture. (Corbett and Slee 2000: 134)

The emphasis here on celebrating differences is important. Effective practitioners embrace the unique characteristics of each child. Thus, 'difference' is seen as a positive aspect that is to be embraced and celebrated. Corbett and Slee emphasise that effective inclusion requires practitioners to continually evaluate and reflect on the provision that is available. Therefore, inclusion should be seen as a *process* rather than a *product*. New children entering a setting will have different needs that should be met.

Effective practitioners will develop positive relationships with parents and carers to establish the needs of each child. The family is a rich source of information and information gleaned at this point will enable practitioners to provide appropriate provision for the child from the outset. Inclusion demands that practitioners reflect on their own value system. Inclusion and values go very much hand in hand. Early observational assessments from both home and the setting are important, as it through these observations that barriers to learning and participation can be identified. Conversations with parents, carers and grandparents should also be documented and added to the child's learning journal. These conversations may help practitioners to establish the needs of the child and identify barriers to learning and participation.

Inclusion requires practitioners to embrace the *social model of disability*. Within this model, the social world is seen as disabling and disability is seen as a social construct. The social model essentially distinguishes between *disability* and *impairment*. The key assumption within the social model is that *within-child factors* (impairments) only become disabling in certain situations and the disability only arises as a result of society's failure to make adjustments to provision. In most cases, appropriate changes can be made to provision so that those children with impairments are able to participate and achieve. According to Tregaskis (2002: 457), 'the social model of disability has been an emancipatory force in the lives of many disabled people.' This model challenges the *medical model,* which locates the source of disablement as within the body, thus essentially constructing individuals as 'victims' and blaming them for any lack of participation or achievement.

- How can the social model be applied in early years settings?

- To what extent does diagnostic assessment, which is often used by outside agencies, reflect a medical model of disability?

Corbett (2001) emphasises that inclusion must not be based on a 'dump and hope' (p13) model. She argues that 'inclusive education has to be workable and to give good value in terms of a quality learning experience for all' (Corbett 2001: 13). This is an important point. Inclusion therefore places an onus on settings to adapt their policies and practices to cater for the needs of the child. There is no onus on the child to fit in with the requirements of the setting. The key to achieving an inclusive ethos is *flexibility*. Policies, practices and routines need to be flexible and changed if they do not meet the needs of specific learners.

According to Florian (1998: 107), 'the inclusion of *all* pupils in mainstream schools is part of an international human rights agenda which calls for the full inclusion of all people with disabilities in all aspects of life.' The disability rights movement has been instrumental in emphasising the rights of disabled people to fully participate and take advantage of the opportunities offered in mainstream education and employment. According to Thomas et al.,

Although inclusion has won partly because of evidence from educational research ... it has won mainly because it is *right* that it should have done so. Arguments for inclusion are principled ones, stemming from concern for human rights. (Thomas et al. 1998: 5)

The writers emphasise here that inclusion, rights and values are intertwined. Therefore, it seems logical that practitioners must reflect on their own values before thinking seriously about inclusion. Your own values will affect the commitment you put into developing inclusive practices. Values are difficult to change and are shaped by a range of factors, including one's own background, upbringing and personal experiences of schooling. As a bare minimum, practitioners need to be able to demonstrate that they hold non-discriminatory values and embrace the principles of equal opportunities. In order to work in an inclusive way, you will need to embrace a social model perspective. You will need to be highly reflective and be willing to make adaptations to your practices in order to enable children to be able to participate and achieve.

Often the effective approaches for children with Special educational needs (SEN) are also effective approaches for all children. Strategies such as visual timetables to support children with autistic spectrum disorder may also be valuable for many more children without SEN. The key to success is to be willing to try new strategies and to be prepared to evaluate them. Observational assessment is crucial. Through observations, you will be able to decide whether a particular strategy or intervention has worked well. You will be able to evaluate the impact of the strategy or intervention in terms of outcomes or achievements. Remember that progress may be evident in the form of very small steps. Multi-sensory approaches to support children with cognition and learning needs may benefit many more children, and strategies to support children with behavioural, emotional and social developmental needs will need to be trialled and evaluated on a regular basis. Careful observational assessments will enable you to evaluate how well children have responded to specific interventions and therefore practitioners may well find that a cycle of *plan, do* and *review* is useful. The key point to remember is that no one will expect you to plan interventions alone. You will be expected to be able to work in partnership with other staff in the setting, with parents and carers, and with other agencies. Each party will be able to support you throughout the planning process. You should listen carefully to the recommended strategies suggested by staff representing different agencies. These professionals will carefully explain the strategies, which you can then implement and evaluate. A home–school diary will be invaluable to enable you to maintain a regular dialogue with parents and careers. They will want to know how their child has responded to specific strategies and a diary will facilitate this sharing of information.

Steps towards the development of inclusive education can be traced back to the Warnock Report (DES 1978). This recommended the policy of *integration*. The 1981 Education Act introduced the Statement of Special Educational Needs. This provided funding to support the most vulnerable children in mainstream settings. Further advances towards inclusion were made in the 1990s with the *Salamanca Statement* (UNESCO 1994), which asked countries around the globe to subscribe to the principle of inclusive education by enrolling all children in mainstream environments unless there were significant reasons for not doing so. Legislation now makes it unlawful for educational settings to discriminate on the basis of disability. The Special Educational Needs and Disability Act (SENDA) 2001 made it unlawful for settings to discriminate against disabled children in either the arrangements for admission or curriculum provision. This legislation emphasises that all settings should take 'reasonable steps' to ensure that children with disabilities have the same opportunities to participate in the education and other services provided. In addition, this legislation stresses the need for settings to plan strategically how accessibility can be increased. The *Code of Practice for Special Educational Needs* (DfES 2001) stresses the need to involve children and parents in the assessment processes and the importance of collecting the views of the child at key review points.

The government's strategy for SEN, *Removing Barriers to Achievement* (DfES 2004a) focuses on:

- Early intervention.

- Removing barriers to learning.

- Raising expectations and achievement.

- Delivering improvements in partnership.

This strategy is part of the *Every Child Matters* agenda (HM Government 2004), which promotes the principles of inclusive education. These principles have been embraced in the new Early Years Foundation Stage (EYFS) framework. Early intervention and working in partnership with a range of agencies, including parents are key elements of inclusive practices.

 Reflective Activity

Split into two groups to discuss one of the following reflective tasks:

1. Think carefully about the impact of poverty and social deprivation on children's learning. Why are children who are born into poverty at risk of underachievement? Discuss your ideas with your colleagues in class. How can you develop an effective partnership with parents and carers to improve outcomes for the child? Use the information on the Joseph Rowntree Foundation website to inform your understanding. The website is listed at the end of this chapter.
2. Think carefully with your colleagues about the impact of gender and ethnicity on children's learning. How might it impact on outcomes for children and what research has been undertaken in this area?

Present your findings to the rest of the group.

Key Point

*   Effective practitioners celebrate difference and diversity and view diversity as a positive feature. Ensure your classroom environment reflects a range of cultural images and resources and think carefully about how provision areas can be developed to reflect difference and diversity.

The Common Assessment Framework

The Common Assessment Framework (CAF) is an assessment of a child's holistic needs. A CAF might be completed if there are concerns about a child's progress or behaviour. Additionally, a CAF might also be completed if there are concerns about the child's home circumstances. The CAF reduces the need for different agencies from education, social services and health to carry out separate assessments. The purpose of the CAF is to facilitate the sharing of information across the agencies.

Team around the child: multi-agency working

The *Every Child Matters* agenda promotes effective multi-agency working and sharing of information between agencies. Several agencies may be supporting a child with SEN, so the efficient sharing of information across agencies can lead to earlier intervention and support. Children living in poverty may be at risk of underachievement, and effective information sharing across agencies can help to raise outcomes for these children. The team around the child may be made up of teachers, parents and practitioners from health, education and social services who all work together to raise outcomes for individual children. The current emphasis on multi-agency working brings challenges with it. Effective practitioners are able to break down professional boundaries and focus on the holistic child. Teachers in particular have traditionally operated within an educational paradigm rather than a social paradigm. The current emphasis on *educare* asks practitioners to think more carefully about the holistic child. Teachers are now required to think about children's social and emotional development and the impact of this on learning. Practitioners can gain valuable information from other agencies to help them implement different strategies to support individual children.

A child who is hungry, thirsty or tired will find it difficult to learn (Maslow's work is useful here). If education practitioners are aware of the impact of social deprivation on learning, then simple adjustments can be made to practice which might help to break down some of these barriers to participation and learning. This might be a simple adjustment such as providing a quiet place for a child to sleep during the day or providing children with breakfast before they start the day. Professionals within a multi-disciplinary team will be responsible for making day-to-day assessments of children. It is important for professionals to share their assessments with other professionals in the team and to provide advice and support to front-line practitioners in relation to children's targets and strategies that can be used to help children achieve their next steps in learning. The views of parents, carers and children should be listened to and acted upon.

The lead professional

The lead professional is the nominated person responsible for coordinating the involvement of different agencies. The lead professional also organises the multi-professional meetings as well as maintaining regular communication with the family. The lead professional may be a nominated representative from education, health or social services.

 Case Study: Nursery: Suzie and Stephen, aged 3–4 years

Read the following case study and think carefully about how problems with early language development might impact negatively on learning in other areas of learning.

Bob has the care of his two children, Suzie aged 4 years and Stephen aged 3 years. His partner now lives with someone else and works full time. The children visit their mother on Saturdays but do not stay overnight.

The early years Special Educational Needs Coordinator (SENCO) had discussed with Bob her concerns about Suzie's language development. Her early years key worker had noticed that she had some communication problems linked to behaviour issues. Bob said that he had some concerns about Stephen's behaviour, as he displayed tantrums at home that continued until he was sick or he stopped from exhaustion. Bob had not mentioned this before, as he felt that he would be admitting that he was not coping. Stephen had been attending the nursery at the children's centre for a month and had been quiet and withdrawn. He did not mix with the other children, preferring to play in the adventure tunnel or the playhouse alone. He did enjoy outside play.

The SENCO suggested a CAF and explained the process to Bob. Whilst the assessment was in process, Bob revealed that he had been under stress due to the childcare commitments, financial worries and feeling isolated. He reported that the children were particularly difficult when they returned from a visit with their mother.

The SENCO completed the common assessment alongside Bob and the health visitor who had been involved with the family. A Team Around the Child (TAC) meeting was organised and other agencies were invited. The children's mother agreed to attend. The other agencies that attended included Speech and Language, Fathers Together, Behaviour Support and Educational Psychology. The SENCO was the lead professional who coordinated the interventions and multi-agency involvement. She gave Bob lots of support

(Continued)

and built a relationship based on trust. She reported that this took time and patience, but it was extremely rewarding and productive. Bob has learnt a wide range of strategies to manage Stephen's behaviour, and these are consistent with the strategies used in the setting. The Behaviour Support service provided Bob with constant advice. As a result, Stephen is more settled both at home and in the setting. In addition, as a result of the CAF, Suzie was able to receive support from a speech and language therapist. The early intervention, triggered by her concerns for Suzie, had improved the outcomes for the whole family.

- Do you think the family break-up was significant in impacting on Stephen's behaviour? If so, why might the break-up impact on his behaviour?
- How did the TAC meeting support Bob?
- Can you think of any issues associated with the idea of a Team Around the Child?
- How might language deprivation impact on subsequent attainment in reading and writing? You might want to research further into this.

Labelling

It has been argued that categorising children produces 'frozen, atomised photographs' and 'fragmented snapshots' (Billington 2000: 90), which highlight 'frozen, individualised and pathologized differences' (Billington 2000: 91). Thus, the labels that are attached to them through diagnosis define children's identities. Billington's point is important. There is a danger that practitioners might assume that all autistic children have the same traits (the image is frozen) and will respond to the same strategies and interventions in the same way. Effective practitioners will find individual strategies that work with specific children. Two autistic children may display very different characteristics and respond differently to specific strategies.

Key Point

- Effective practitioners do not try to 'normalise' children. Instead they embrace the individuality of all children.

The importance of assessment

Ongoing assessments will help to identify specific difficulties and needs. It is important that you recognise the small steps which children take and understand that it may take some children longer to achieve specific milestones. Regular assessment is crucial, as it will help you to identify what children can do and this will aid future planning. As discussed in Chapter 8, it is important to include the voice of the child and their parents or carers in your assessments. Steps in learning may need to be broken down further so that children are able to experience success. Children with SEN must experience a sense of achievement in order to preserve their self-esteem. For these children (as with all children), the child's learning journey provides a vehicle for celebrating these achievements. Learning journeys for these children need to document the very small steps that they may have taken and these should be regularly discussed with each child and parent or carer. The learning journey makes the progress visible and public and this will help to foster a sense of confidence. Rich observational assessments will provide information to practitioners about children's learning needs. For some children, it will be necessary to modify activities so that achievement can be demonstrated in a diverse range of ways.

The guidelines that follow are not meant to be prescriptive. They simply provide practitioners with some general pointers, which they might find useful. We are not trying to categorise children or put them into boxes of common characteristics. Assessment should help to identify next steps in learning and this should inform planning and intervention. Assessment *during* and *after* interventions will inform future planning. Practitioners are therefore recommended to follow a cycle of assessment, planning, intervention, further assessment and review. Effective practitioners will implement strategies to support children's individual needs. Your assessments of how individual children respond to these strategies will determine whether strategies are successful or not. Less successful interventions will need to be abandoned or rethought.

Children with English as an additional language (EAL)

Look, listen and note

Children with EAL may find it difficult to stay on task, particularly if they have not understood the task. They may not participate in activities and they may be reluctant to make contributions. All of these difficulties could be due to difficulties with comprehending English.

Development of effective practice

Practitioners need to accompany verbal instructions with pictures. Signs, symbols, ICT and pictures can be used to accompany verbal instructions and verbal teaching. Notices in the setting should reflect the child's home language, and letters and notices to parents should be available in the home language. The child will benefit from kinaesthetic approaches to teaching and learning. The provision areas should reflect children's cultural backgrounds and texts are available in different languages.

Challenges and dilemmas

Practitioners need to respect parents and carers who may communicate with the child in his or her home language. Additionally, effective practitioners may teach the child's home language to other children so that all children are able to communicate with the child in the home language and English. It is important not to devalue the home language but to embrace its use.

Children with autistic spectrum disorder

Look, listen and note

Observe to see whether the child has difficulties with (1) social interaction; (2) social communication, including verbal and non-verbal communication; and (3) use of imagination. Lorna Wing termed this the *triad of impairments*. Typically, children with autistic spectrum disorders prefer to be alone and avoid eye contact. Children with Asperger's syndrome may develop obsessions. Children with autism may be upset if their routine suddenly changes.

Development of effective practice

Ensure that visual cues are available. This could be through the use of a daily visual timetable or a visual communication system. You may consider integrating the child's interests or obsessions into the curriculum.

Challenges and dilemmas

Children with autism may develop aggressive traits and they may be prone to tantrums. Ensure there is a quiet space where children can go if they need to calm down. Build a positive relationship with parents and carers and share behaviour strategies. Work in collaboration with outside agencies, including the local authority. Do not try to force social interaction and social communication. This will need to be planned very gradually. Celebrate the child's uniqueness and view autism as a positive aspect of the child's personality rather than something tragic. Do not force the child to make eye contact with you. Teach the other children about autism and give them strategies for managing potentially volatile situations.

Children with behavioural, emotional and social difficulties

Look, listen and note

Observe to see whether children are easily distracted. They may not persist with activities. They may have low self-esteem and they may find it difficult to stay on task. Sometimes children with social, emotional and behavioural difficulties may find it difficult to develop positive relationships with their peers and they may test the rules within the setting.

Development of effective practice

It is essential that practitioners start to develop positive relationships with parents and carers. Backing from home will be essential and there needs to be consistent approaches and expectations between home and the setting. A home–school diary will be an invaluable tool for facilitating effective communication with parents and carers. Practitioners and parents will need to meet regularly to discuss progress and to agree new targets together. Practitioners should adopt a collaborative approach. The information provided by the parent or carer could be invaluable in terms of explaining why the child may have difficulties. The difficulties could relate to home circumstances. Additionally, it is important that practitioners distinguish between the behaviour and the child – it is the behaviour that is not acceptable and practitioners need to demonstrate to the child that he or she is still valued and included in the setting. This will help to maintain the child's self-esteem. Targets need to be set to enable the child to make progress. These need to be realistic and achievable. Progress towards the targets needs to be reviewed regularly. Practitioners should consult with the child on a regular basis to discuss their behaviour. Practitioners should actively seek the views of children and their parents or carers. Effective practitioners need to find out what the child enjoys doing, and wherever possible the curriculum should be tailored around the interests of the child. Thus, practitioners need to engage in a process of reflection and they need to be prepared to modify practice to meet the needs of the child. This is a social model perspective. Effective practitioners view behavioural issues as developmental; that is, they hold the view that children with difficulties are still learning the accepted social codes. Effective practitioners take active steps to include rather than exclude and strategies to support the child are planned, implemented and evaluated on a regular basis in collaboration with children, parents, carers and external agencies.

Challenges and dilemmas

In a busy setting, challenging behaviour can be extremely stressful. Sometimes it is difficult to remain positive and it can become physically tiring. Establishing effective and positive relationships with parents and carers is not always as straightforward as it sounds. This is especially true when there is a conflict between home values and values in the setting. Another key challenge is that other children in the setting need to learn strategies for managing the behaviour of children with social, emotional and behavioural difficulties. They also need to realise that systems for managing behaviour have to be applied flexibly to meet the needs of individual children.

Children with hearing impairments

Look, listen and note

Children with hearing impairments may have difficulties with speech and sentence construction. They may lack participation, especially in large group sessions and they may appear to lack concentration. They may find it difficult to follow instructions and they may lack the ability to stay on a task, particularly if they do not understand what they are required to do. The symptoms may vary depending on the type of hearing impairment.

Development of effective practice

If children are using sign language or picture exchange communication systems, then effective practitioners will also learn to communicate using these systems. Practitioners should speak clearly and slowly and ensure that they face children when speaking directly to them. Verbal instructions can also be provided visually. Effective practitioners make good use of visual and kinaesthetic approaches in their teaching in order to remove barriers to learning created by auditory approaches. Effective practitioners maintain good communication with parents and external agencies, and strategies will be shared, implemented and evaluated.

Challenges and dilemmas

Effective practitioners need to encourage all other children in the setting, to communicate effectively with children with hearing impairments. In inclusive settings, children learn to use sign language if this is a child's prime method of communication. Children also need to learn other ways of communicating with a hearing-impaired child and the practitioner can model these.

Children with visual impairments

Look, listen and note

These children may have poor hand–eye coordination. They may show signs of clumsiness and they may find it difficult to focus on information presented visually.

Development of effective practice

Effective practitioners need to ensure that children with visual impairments are familiar with the layout of the setting and any potential risks. The layout should be planned carefully so that risks are minimised. Labels, signs and storybooks can be produced in Braille (or large text), and Braille keyboards for computers are also available. Children with visual impairment will benefit from a kinaesthetic learning experience. The provision within EYFS settings is ideal in terms of providing children with tactile experiences. Practitioners should take advice from the visual impairment service and the child's parents.

Challenges and dilemmas

If the child works with an additional adult, it be essential that the child be encouraged to be independent in his/her learning. Planning should take into account the need for developing increased independence.

Children with speech, language and communication difficulties

Look, listen and note

Children with speech, language and communication difficulties may have difficulties with oral word and sentence formation. They may find it difficult to express their thoughts. Additionally, these children may have low self-esteem. They may also have difficulties with phonological awareness and early sound discrimination.

Development of effective practice

Practitioners may find it useful to discuss effective strategies with the speech and language service within the local authority. Instructions might need to be presented visually as well as orally, through the use of pictures.

Challenges and dilemmas

Practitioners should ensure that children feel fully included in the setting. They should regularly interact with all children and have conversations with them. They should take steps to ensure that other children in the group include children with speech, language and communication difficulties in play activities.

Children with reading difficulties

Look, listen and note

Children who develop difficulties with reading in the Foundation Stage may have difficulties with early sound discrimination. In addition these children may find it difficult to identify rhyme in the early years. Practitioners should pay close attention to children with speech and language difficulties, or hearing difficulties as these difficulties could impact on the child's ability to hear sounds and pronounce sounds. Practitioners in nursery settings should understand the relationship between early phonological awareness (musical and environmental sound discrimination, rhyme, and alliteration) and children's subsequent reading development. A child who finds it difficult to distinguish between a high and a low sound may have problems with phonology in later years. Likewise, a child who finds it difficult to identify the different sounds of a drum, a tambourine and a cymbal may have difficulty in distinguishing between the phonemes in later years.

Development of effective practice

Effective practitioners provide children with lots of rich experiences in developing early phonological awareness. These children need to be exposed to rhyming games and early sound discrimination activities. Towards the end of the Foundation Stage, practitioners will start to introduce children to the phonemes represented by specific graphemes in the alphabet. This needs to be done by a multi-sensory approach by visual, auditory and kinaesthetic methods. For all children it is important to experience writing letters in the sand, water, dough, clay and soil. However, this approach is even more important for those children who have difficulties with sound discrimination. Writing letters in the air, tracing letters on the palm of the hand, or feeling letters made from different, textured materials will provide children with rich experiences. In addition, practitioners should think carefully about ways in which the provision areas in the setting can be enhanced in order to make them print rich. For example, large letters or grapheme cards can be placed in the free writing area. Letters can be placed in the sand or water. Practitioners should make the reading area exciting by including texts that appeal to specific children. Books should be attractive, with covers facing outward and practitioners should regularly work alongside children in these areas so that they are able to model the process of being a reader or a writer. If children see adults reading for pleasure, then this might motivate them to go and pick up a book. Effective practitioners set short-term targets. These are arrived at through a deep knowledge of the steps which children progress through when learning to read. Effective practitioners create an effective environment where print is embedded. The importance of a language-rich environment cannot be overstated. This includes the importance of a talk-rich environment through creating effective role-play areas, the use of drama, and listening areas. Effective practitioners understand the interrelationship between speaking, listening, reading and writing. Effective practitioners develop effective relationships with parents and carers, who then support children in their literacy development at home. Simple language games can be sent home for parents to share with children. Parents and carers can draw children's attention to environmental print and encourage their child to join the local library. Effective practitioners consult the child regularly about the types of books they enjoy reading.

Challenges and dilemmas

Some children will have a language-impoverished environment at home. Additionally, some parents or carers might not value reading and be reluctant to support the child in his/her reading development. Practitioners should not assume that parents and carers are able to read or write, and this needs to be handled with sensitivity.

Gifted and talented children

Look, listen and note

Gifted children may have received lots of support from parents and carers at home, but this is not always the case. They tend to be academically able and they pick up ideas and concepts quickly. However, they may prefer solitary play and this can lead to their not forming attachments with their peers, thus resulting in isolation. Their reasoning skills may be good and they may have developed speech. Gifted children may be emotionally immature. They may understand the implications of traumatic situations but may not be able to put that information into context.

Development of effective practice

Careful assessment of the child's knowledge and skills will enable practitioners to plan the next steps for gifted children. Effective practitioners develop very positive relationships with parents and carers. Activities need to be challenging and pitched at an appropriate level. Play activities may need to be tightly structured on occasions in order to maximise learning opportunities. However, such children should be provided with opportunities to play with their peers in order to aid their social development. Practitioners will need to be familiar with the content of the National Curriculum in order to extend their learning further. Practitioner subject knowledge is therefore very important.

Challenges and dilemmas

Some children may display characteristics that mask their giftedness. Therefore practitioners may fail to identify a gifted child from a socially deprived background, especially if that same child has behavioural issues and frequently comes into the setting late. This is an example of stereotyping and practitioners must realise that gifted children can be born into different social and cultural backgrounds.

 Case Study: Playgroup: Adam, aged 2 years

Read the following case study and think about the importance of effective parent partnership in the assessment of children with SEN. Think what the barriers to establishing an effective partnership might be.

(Continued)

Adam and his mum came to playgroup for three sessions. Mum sat alongside Adam as he tentatively explored the garage. They had a snack, but not a drink. They did not stay for full sessions. When Mum decided to leave Adam, he was vaguely aware that she was going. During observations, Adam seemed to show that he played with a small range of resources. He screamed loudly when he thought others would take the resources he was playing with. He would tolerate his key person and her interventions but on the whole seemed to allow her to be there. A feeder cup helped him to have a good drink each morning. A watchful eye to anticipate danger prevented many a serious accident. When enhancements were added to provision or the layout of the setting changed, it seemed that Adam was unsure. He needed to approach changes carefully and be reassured of his freedom to access the toilet or the snack table when he was ready. Adam spoke in sounds not words. He was nearly 3 years old.

The key person in playgroup talked regularly with Mum. Together they updated the 'All about Me' book. It took time. Through observation, the key person had some examples of activities that Adam enjoyed. There were some children he sought out to play next to, and the feeder cup was being filled independently. Samples of the sounds and the contexts in which they had been spoken were discussed. The photographs and careful notes made Mum smile. They really knew him at playgroup. The referral to speech and language set Adam and his family off on a journey that included visits to the paediatrician and meetings with the Portage team. Throughout the process, the playgroup key person and sometimes the SENCO would talk things through and work out how advice and support could work in their playgroup. The committee ensured that there were appropriate numbers of staff, and the local authority provided support through additional funding. The toy library was a good source of ideas for equipment. Things with lights and sounds really attracted Adam. By the time Adam was ready for school, there was a statement of SEN in place.

Visits to Mum's chosen school took place and practitioners from the school visited playgroup. Observations formed the basis of the discussion. Mum felt confident to share the photos she and the playgroup had put together. It helped to have a visual prompt. The Individual Education Plan to support Adam's transition was in place ready for his start in school.

- How did the practitioners in the setting develop an effective and trustful relationship with Adam's mother?
- Why was the 'All about Me' book so effective?

- What are the issues associated with transition and how did this setting take steps to make the transition smoother for Adam and his mother?
- What are the barriers to effective parent partnership in the assessment of children with SEN?

🔑 Key Points

- Effective practitioners develop strategies for individual children, not strategies for a designated label.
- Effective practitioners develop and evaluate strategies in collaboration with parents, carers and the children. Intervention strategies can be evaluated through careful observational assessments of children's responses to these.

This chapter has emphasised the importance of careful observational assessment as a tool to identify specific difficulties and children's responses to particular intervention strategies. For children with SEN, it is vital that parents or carers be involved fully in the assessment process. Practitioners should provide them with frequent opportunities to evaluate strategies, and parents or carers should be encouraged to set new targets in collaboration with practitioners in the setting. Children's achievements at home and in the setting should be celebrated and included in the child's learning journey. Learning journeys should be frequently discussed with parents, carers and children. Small achievements should be documented and celebrated, thus helping to maintain the child's self-esteem. Relationships with both children and parents or carers should be highly positive and non-confrontational. As a practitioner, you need to recognise and value the contribution that significant others and the child can make to the assessment process. Learning journeys should reflect the voices of all key stakeholders and document what the child can do. Effective practitioners identify barriers to learning and participation and make reasonable adjustments to aspects of practice. Observe, listen to and note children's difficulties and responses to interventions and strategies. Talk to children about what interests them and build this into curriculum planning.

Reflective Activity

Ruth and her four children have recently moved into the area and Ruth does not have any family or friends here. The children are 2, 4, 5 and 10 years old. Her partner left 12 months ago and has not made contact with Ruth or the children since. The three elder children are from a previous relationship. Ruth has a serious, physically debilitating, medical condition and is waiting for transplant surgery. Ruth's only other relative, her stepmother, lives 200 miles away in Manchester and doesn't have a car. The family live in a three-bedroom, privately rented house. The house is in a rundown condition and the garden unfit for the children to play in. Ruth is extremely loving and caring of all her four children and is doing well in maintaining stability despite recent changes. Her two eldest children are registered in school but are not attending well due to Ruth's health. Ruth's neighbour advised her to approach the local children's centre for support.

The early years practitioner in the children's centre described the Common Assessment Framework to Ruth and she consented to information being shared with all involved agencies. CAFs were completed for all the children and a TAC was formed that supported and represented the whole family. The TAC worked collaboratively, requesting support where needed and involving other agencies appropriately. The early years practitioner became the lead practitioner. She collaborated with the primary school and the healthcare staff to engage other agencies to support the family. The early years practitioner received appropriate support and supervision around her role as lead practitioner and was encouraged to 'think family'.

The TAC worked collaboratively, requesting support where needed and involving others in a timely and appropriate way.

- In the above case study, how do the home circumstances impact on learning and development?
- To what extent can the TAC empower or disempower families?
- How does the assessment process focus on children's holistic development?

Further Reading

Ross-Watt, F. (2005) 'Inclusion and the Early Years: From Rhetoric to Reality', *Child Care in Practice*, 11 (2), 103–118.

Useful Websites

www.csie.org.uk

- The Centre for Studies in Inclusive Education website includes a wealth of information related to inclusion, including definitions of inclusion, current legislation, research and publications. This site will be useful for all students who have to produce assignments on inclusion.

www.everychildmatters.gov.uk

- The *Every Child Matters* website includes extensive information about different aspects of the *Every Child Matters* agenda, including the outcomes framework, safeguarding, parent partnership, information sharing across agencies, and multi-disciplinary working. This site will support you in your academic studies and your professional practice.

www.jrf.org.uk

- The Joseph Rowntree Foundation site includes a wealth of research on the links between social deprivation and underachievement and the underachievement of specific groups of learners. This site will be excellent for supporting your academic studies.

10

The early years foundation stage and beyond

Jonathan Glazzard

Chapter Objectives

- Address a consistent approach to assessment between the Early Years Foundation Stage (EYFS) and Key Stage 1.
- Provide examples of effective practice through case studies.
- Provide a framework for assessment that addresses the current focus on teacher assessment in Key Stage 1.

This chapter introduces students to effective transition arrangements as children move from the Early Years Foundation Stage into the Year 1 setting. We consider what effective assessment might look like in Year 1 in view of the current focus on teacher assessment in Key Stage 1. Whilst this chapter focuses on approaches to assessment in Year 1, we stress here that effective assessment should be developed throughout Key Stages 1 and 2 and that best practice will reflect the philosophy towards assessment adopted in the Foundation Stage. Schools might wish to consider embedding effective assessment processes in Year 1 before rolling these approaches out across the school. Current policy places an increased emphasis on the importance of regular formative assessment in Key Stage 1, with a reduced emphasis on formal assessments. We welcome this change in direction. It is hoped that this philosophy will be adopted as the approach to assessment across the primary age range in the coming years. Practitioners in the Foundation Stage are the leading experts within this field and should be willing to share their philosophy and practice with colleagues across the school.

Continuing the assessment journey

Throughout the country, Year 1 practitioners annually receive EYFSP data, ready to begin the autumn term for their learners. This data provides a summary of individual attainment in the six areas of learning for all children as they exit the EYFS. It is vital that this data becomes a working document for all Year 1 practitioners if they are to effectively build on attainment to date.

Effective Year 1 practitioners must:

• Understand current national attainment expectations at the end of the EYFS (profile scale points). Without this knowledge, Year 1 practitioners will be unable to identify learners who are working below, above or within national expectations.

• Be familiar with and understand the EYFS framework. This will be essential for the practitioner to plan next steps in learning and support each child in working towards evidencing attainment against the National Curriculum.

• Fully understand when evidence of attainment measured against the EYFS framework and profile also evidences attainment against the National Curriculum. This is the point at which attainment can be effectively measured against the National Curriculum. Children's next steps can then be planned using the National Curriculum and non-statutory guidance. This includes the National Strategies and materials that support these, including the use of the APP (*Assessing Pupils' Progress*) materials.

Continuing the learning journey

At the end of the EYFS, children's learning is summarised in the EYFSP (QCA 2008). Many EYFS practitioners have embraced the principle of frequent observational assessment as an ongoing process for identifying individual achievements and future learning needs. It is possible that children will enter Year 1 without having achieved the Early Learning Goals. For these children it is important that Year 1 practitioners continue to track children's learning and development against the EYFSP. Essentially, children who have not achieved the Early Learning Goals by the end of the Foundation Stage are not ready to progress to the National Curriculum.

The implications of continuing the learning and assessment journey into Year 1 mean that practitioners in Year 1 must adopt similar pedagogical approaches to those used in the Foundation Stage. Practitioners who move children onto the National Curriculum too quickly risk missing out major developmental milestones which children need to go through in order to provide a firm foundation for subsequent learning.

Key Point

- EYFS and Key Stage 1 practitioners should be familiar with both the EYFS framework and the National Curriculum, to ensure continuity in learning and a smooth transition for all children between the two frameworks. Practitioners must identify next steps in learning by referring to the curriculum framework that best meets the needs of the child. Children work both above and below national expectations. Year 1 children may still need to have their learning needs met through the EYFS framework. Likewise, a high-attaining child in the Foundation Stage may need to be assessed against the EYFSP and the National Curriculum. This would be particularly relevant for children achieving scale point 9.

Continuing pedagogical approaches

A sudden transition to a more formal learning environment in Year 1 can have a detrimental impact on children's dispositions and attitudes. In the Foundation Stage, children in effective settings have experienced a broad, rich, play-based curriculum. They will have been provided with frequent opportunities to initiate their own learning. Children will have therefore been provided with a substantial element of choice over the tasks they have undertaken. In effective settings, children are encouraged to select their own resources and put them away. They will also have been given freedom over how long to persist with self-chosen activities. The curriculum is active and responsive to the needs and interests of the children. Excellent practitioners will have supported children in their play by playing with them and scaffolding their learning. Children in the Foundation Stage may be used to not having a fixed seating place. They may not always work at tables. Indeed, in many settings there are not enough table spaces for each child because these are not needed. Children are used to working on the floor and they are used to learning both indoors and outdoors. They are used to working with different children. There is no distinction between work and play because play is the child's learning. In terms of assessment, children in the Foundation Stage are not aware that their learning is being monitored. Assessment is continuous and based on observation. Assessment is always positive and focuses on what children know and can do. This approach to assessment celebrates each child's achievements, thus helping to maintain self-esteem.

Imagine the worst-case scenario. Children have experienced learning and assessment as described above throughout the EYFS. In fact, their experiences should still be reflective of this best practice at the end of the Foundation Stage.

What if...?

Consider the following scenario.

What if these children then start Year 1 at the beginning of the academic year and they are faced with contrasting pedagogical approaches? What if learning suddenly becomes formalised? Now they are learning 'subjects' and doing 'lessons' rather than activities. They are made to sit for long periods of time on the carpet. They mainly do tasks that are directed by the teacher, and they do these at tables. They work in the same groups all day. The resources are laid out for them on their tables. The only time they get to play is when they have finished their work. There is only a cursory attempt at providing a role-play area and the reading area is infrequently used. After they have worked, they are allowed to 'choose' (play). There is clear distinction between work and play. Play is not valued because practitioners do not play and interact with children. Children's learning is monitored through frequent tests and children know they are at being tested. Children know they are at this level or that level, and they know (and are able to articulate) what they need to do to get to the next sublevel.

What do you think the impact of this transition will be on the child?

We have described the worst-case scenario here – a sudden transition to Year 1 which effectively constitutes a rejection of the principles and practices of the EYFS. However, our experiences in visiting a range of Year 1 classes confirm that the scenario described above is very often a reality. We have seen children being taught in sterile and uninspiring environments. We have seen much formal learning and little play-based learning. We have also witnessed children completing worksheet after worksheet in order to evidence the learning that has taken place. In these settings, children fill in one box after another. They put their hand up to ask whether they may get a pencil sharpener. They are dependent on the teacher because he/she will tell them what to do next. These children often lack motivation and sometimes test the boundaries because the learning experience fails to stimulate them.

We are also lucky enough to have experienced some inspirational Year 1 settings. The practitioners in these settings have worked closely with their Foundation Stage colleagues to create stimulating, play-based environments. Assessment is based on observation and provision areas are structured to provide challenging contexts for active learning. The children in these settings are happy and confident. They are independent and engaged with their learning. In these effective settings play is not something which children do after they have completed their work. Play-based learning takes place alongside adult-directed tasks and children interchange between the two. In these settings, the practitioners are able to continue the learning journeys for those children who have not achieved the Early Learning Goals. At the same time, they are able to challenge other children by focusing on the Programmes of Study in the National Curriculum. The National Curriculum can be delivered very effectively through structuring play experiences. However, children will have limited opportunity to achieve the Early Learning Goals through formal learning experiences.

A sudden transition to more formal learning environments can damage children's self-esteem. It can result in children disengaging from the learning process and school in general. Formal learning experiences in Year 1 are not consistent with how young children learn. Children are active learners. Piaget's work informs us of the importance of discovery learning and it is still relevant today. Formal assessment processes such as testing reinforce what children do not know. Testing highlights failure rather than success by indicating to children how far away they are from national norms. Moving children too quickly onto the National Curriculum will result in gaps in learning and important foundations not being laid.

It is very easy to understand why children experience a change in pedagogical approaches upon entry to Year 1. Year 1 practitioners are desperate to get children to achieve age-related National Curriculum norms. They are working within a standards-imposed agenda. They will ultimately have to justify their results, and their performance will be evaluated on the basis of their results. However, we argue in this chapter that it is possible for children to achieve their potential against the National Curriculum through play-based approaches to teaching and learning. It stands to reason that happy, motivated and excited children will achieve more than learners who are disengaged.

We have witnessed the effects of the standards agenda in the final term of the EYFS. We have seen sudden transitions to more whole-class teaching and a switch from an integrated approach to discrete lessons. Undoubtedly, some Foundation Stage practitioners feel the pressure to 'prepare' children for Year 1. This is detrimental to children's learning and denies them their full entitlement to the principles of the Foundation Stage. Practitioners should resist the pressure from Year 1 colleagues to adopt more formal approaches, and Year 1 colleagues should adapt their practice to mirror that of the Foundation Stage. This will create a smoother transition, and motivated learners will also achieve higher outcomes in the National Curriculum. The move from an active to a static curriculum should be rejected.

We have witnessed parental resistance to play-based approaches to teaching and learning in some areas. This is particularly the case in some of our middle-class areas, where parents seem keen for their children to be learning in more formal ways. This is challenging for practitioners to address, but they have a role to play in helping parents to understand the value and importance of play-based learning. We stress that children deserve a rich, active and broad curriculum throughout the Foundation Stage and the primary years. The current shift to teacher assessment in Key Stage 1 is promising in that colleagues in Year 1 are now able to adopt similar approaches to assessment to those in the Foundation Stage. Evidence of children's achievements can therefore be collected through:

- Photographic evidence.

- Samples of recorded work.

- Long observations.

- Short observations.

- Digital audio evidence.

- Video/DVD evidence.

Practitioners in Year 1 should collect the evidence of children's achievements into individual learning journeys in order to validate their judgements. A sample of the assessments should be internally and externally moderated (within schools and between schools) to ensure the accuracy of the practitioners' judgements.

Working effectively with colleagues, parents and children

Establishing effective transition arrangements is a key priority, and it will be useful for Year 1 practitioners to spend time in the Foundation Stage observing the children who are due to move into Year 1. It is important that they develop a thorough knowledge of the child's holistic development so that they can continue the child's learning journey in Year 1. Foundation Stage practitioners are advised to share their assessments of the child's learning and development with Year 1 colleagues. This includes sharing the Foundation Stage profile data and discussing the child's next steps and sharing the evidence that contributes to the judgements made against the EYFSP. We also recommend that practitioners working in the EYFS share their philosophy of assessment with their colleagues in Key Stage 1.

We recommend that Year 1 practitioners should spend time talking to the parents of the children they are going to receive. Parents welcome the opportunity to build up a relationship and rapport prior to transition, and they may be anxious about their child moving into the Year 1 setting. They may be concerned that the work will be too difficult for their child, they may be anxious about whether their child will be happy, and they may have perceptions about the pedagogical approaches adopted in Year 1. Many of their preconceptions might exist as due to parents' personal experiences of school. The meeting with parents will provide a valuable opportunity for Year 1 practitioners to reassure parents so they are then able to develop a sense of trust.

Spending time talking to the children is time well spent. Year 1 practitioners are advised to find out about the child's interests, likes and dislikes. They can then use this information to start planning a curriculum that meets the needs of individual learners. We recommend that Year 1 practitioners visit the children in the EYFS setting and also allocate some time for the children to spend some time in Year 1. Best practice is for Year 1 practitioners to adopt similar pedagogical approaches to those used in the Foundation Stage. However, there are likely to be slight differences in systems and procedures and it is helpful to prepare the children for these changes.

Through a thorough knowledge of children's learning, development and interests at the end of the Foundation Stage, Year 1 practitioners will be in a good position to plan each child's learning journey. It is essential that children's learning and development is tracked against the EYFSP if children have not achieved the Early Learning Goals. Effective play-based approaches to learning, including a balance between child-initiated and adult-led learning, will provide an ideal context for tracking children's learning against the profile in Year 1. At the same time, these approaches will also allow other children to demonstrate achievement against the National Curriculum.

 Reflective Activity

You have recently qualified as an early years practitioner working in a Foundation Stage setting. Children in Year 1 and Year 2 are

(Continued)

assessed as an ongoing process but test papers are frequently the assessment tools of choice. How would you begin to work with your colleagues to support the philosophy for effective assessment described in this chapter? Consider that the national agenda now supports the use of formative observational assessment. Also be aware that the most accurate assessments are those undertaken when children are applying previously taught skills and knowledge in an independent context. Consider the limitations of formal approaches to assessment and the benefits of assessing children's learning within meaningful contexts.

Key Point

- EYFS practitioners should work collaboratively with Key Stage 1 practitioners in developing systems that are transferable between the two age phases.

Effective assessment in Year 1

Year 1 practitioners need to understand what effective assessment systems might look like. The current emphasis on teacher assessment in Key Stage 1 means that practitioners in Key Stage 1 need to build up a bank of evidence to validate their judgements about children's attainment. There is a focus now on formative assessment rather than summative assessment and there is less emphasis on the Statutory Assessment Test scores at the end of Year 2. Therefore it is recommended that throughout Key Stage 1 all practitioners involved in supporting children's learning contribute to a learning journey. Decisions will need to be taken in terms of how to organise the learning journeys. Some practitioners may prefer to organise the learning journey into subject areas (focusing on the National Curriculum core subjects) but others may prefer a more integrated approach.

What information should go in the learning journey? Essentially, practitioners should select samples of evidence to include in the learning journey. These should be selected from the child's independent work. It is not necessary to include every piece of evidence, and practitioners should select the pieces of evidence which best reflect the child's abilities. This might include samples of writing throughout the year which evidence the progress made. These will need to be levelled against the National Curriculum level descriptors for children working beyond the Early Learning Goals. For those children working within the goals, the samples might be matched against the profile scores. There needs to be evidence that a sample of judgements has been moderated by colleagues within the school and there might also be evidence of external moderation of assessments between schools. Therefore it is recommended that schools work in clusters and hold regular moderation meetings. This will ensure parity between schools. There might be samples of pupils' recorded mathematics work or science work. These will have been assessed against the National Curriculum level descriptors (or the EYFSP for children who have not achieved the Early Learning Goals).

However, samples of recorded work do not tell the whole story. A sample of recorded science work may not evidence the full knowledge, skills and understanding of a child. It is recommended that these samples of work be supplemented with observations of the children working in practical contexts. These observations can provide a deeper insight into a child's thought processes. It is very difficult to assess children's abilities in scientific enquiry without observing their responses to practical science activities. These practical activities could be set up at the end of a topic to assess the learning that has taken place during a topic. They can be independent activities that require children to assimilate their knowledge, skills and understanding of the topic they have been learning about. Observations of children working through mathematical problems can provide a deeper insight into the strategies that they have used, and this information might not be evident in a piece of recorded work. In order to assess children's word-reading skills, practitioners need to observe children reading independently. This might be carried out through the use of a running record, which includes space for practitioners to write notes about the specific reading strategies which children are using.

For some areas of learning, it is impossible to assess children's abilities without observation. For example, in speaking and listening, practitioners need to assess children's attainment in this area by observing them interacting with other children in a range of contexts. Role-play areas will provide a rich context for assessing children's abilities in this area. Mark-making areas provide a context for collecting children's independent writing. In mathematics areas, practitioners can include aspects of mathematics that have previously been taught and modelled in adult-led sessions. Resources can be integrated which link to the work that has previously been introduced. Practitioners can stand back and observe how children use the resources in these areas, and this can constitute an assessment of the child's independent learning. Therefore, it becomes easy to see that it is impossible to disentangle effective assessment from effective pedagogical approaches. A rich classroom environment in Year 1 will provide a very effective context for collecting assessment evidence. Embedding assessment opportunities into the continuous provision provides an opportunity for contextualising assessment. Assessment is therefore not seen as a 'bolt-on' to teaching and learning. It becomes part and parcel of daily classroom practice. Video evidence, photographs or audio recordings provide very rich data. These can be analysed later in terms of the information they provide about children's attainment.

Year 1 practitioners should involve parents as partners in assessment, and parents and carers should be provided with frequent opportunities to contribute to their child's learning journey. Practitioners should regularly share the learning journey with parents, and it should be freely available for parents and children to access and share with each other. Year 1 practitioners should value the learning which takes place at home. Samples of recorded work or parental observations of children's learning at home should be documented in the learning journey. However, it is important not to overload the learning journey, and only the pieces of evidence that illustrate the child's *significant achievements* should be included. It should be a document that children, parents and practitioners can be proud of. It should be well presented with clear judgements of children's achievements. Additional evidence can be stored in separate files, should the local authority wish to scrutinise it.

Key Points

- Practitioners in Key Stage 1 must embed the principles of formative, observational assessment in their daily practice. Effective assessment practices are an ongoing process in both EYFS and Key Stage 1.

- Key Stage 1 practitioners must evidence assessment judgements in a range of ways on a regular basis, particularly in the core subjects, where attainment is reported at the end of the Key Stage. This evidence may include long and short observations of children's learning, children's work, annotated photographs, and video or audio evidence. This evidence can be included in each child's learning journey.
- Examples of evidence from a range of children's learning journeys could be copied and kept in a subject-specific portfolio. The purpose of the portfolio is to evidence the accurate professional judgements of practitioners across all National Curriculum sublevels for the core subjects. This evidence must be moderated both within and between schools and will be moderated by the local authority.

These systems support the effective transfer of EYFS assessment systems into Key Stage 1. Current requirements emphasise and value teacher assessment as the prime tool for judgements related to attainment in both age phases. It is important that practitioners do not develop systems in isolation and that they share good practice. Practitioners need to develop assessment systems that are both meaningful and manageable, and practitioners in effective settings work together as a team to develop and enhance current assessment practices.

 Case Study: Transforming assessment in Key Stage 1

Read the following case study and think about the challenges that might be involved with transforming assessment processes in Key Stage 1.

School X had developed very strong and effective systems for assessment in the EYFS. The practitioners had developed systems, which had been closely monitored and moderated by the local authority, the senior management team and local partner schools. In the Foundation Stage, the emphasis was on the use of formative observational assessments of children's independent learning. All

(Continued)

practitioners were familiar with the EYFS framework and profile and were competent and confident in identifying children's next steps for all six areas of learning. There was a range of both planned and incidental, as well as both long and short, observations. Practitioner observations were recorded and supported by photographic evidence of children's work and videos. These were clearly linked to the EYFS framework and the EYFSP. Evidence of these assessments was collected in individual learning journeys. These were a working document and shared with parents. The learning journeys were a celebration of individual achievements in the six areas of learning and parents contributed regularly to them. Children's next steps in learning were clearly identified in the learning journeys.

At this time, systems in Key Stage 1 focused heavily on formal methods of assessing children's progress through testing. Children's progress was tested at the end of a unit of work, midyear, and end of year in the core subjects of mathematics, English and science. The concern of the senior management team was that Key Stage 1 practitioners did not have day-to-day knowledge of learners' attainment and were unable to identify the next steps as an ongoing process. It was clear that both the Foundation Stage and Key Stage 1 were using very different approaches for assessment. At this time there were changes to national assessment for Key Stage 1. The emphasis was now placed on teacher assessment (formative assessment) rather than testing.

It was clearly time to continue the assessment journey from EYFS into Key Stage 1. Practitioners in Key Stage 1 joined practitioners in the EYFS setting for two afternoons a week over half a term. They were supported and encouraged to contribute to observational assessments, and they were supported in referencing these assessments to both the EYFS framework and profile. Their judgements were moderated in-house and by partner schools, and the staff in Key Stage 1 were involved in this moderation. As Key Stage 1 practitioner confidence in assessment systems grew, all practitioners moved to the Year 1 setting the following half-term for two afternoons a week. Systems for observation remained the same in terms of evidence collection and moderation. However, judgements about children's learning and the identification of next steps were referenced to published materials relating to National Curriculum level descriptors.

After a term, all practitioners within the EYFS and Key Stage 1 were becoming increasingly skilled in making professional judgements relating to children's achievements against both the EYFS frame-work and the National Curriculum. This was a valuable learning process, enabling all practitioners to make accurate judgements of learners' attainment. The most appropriate framework was used to plan and assess children's learning, and practitioners in both age phases met the needs of the children through their good knowl-edge and appropriate reference to both statutory curriculum frameworks. This effectively met the needs of all children.

Currently, with the advent of APP materials, School X is again reviewing its practice, and attainment in Key Stage 1 is now being measured against the APP materials produced by the National Strategies. Staff in the EYFS are now able to use the APP material to assess the needs of high-attaining children within this phase. This will further positively impact on the effectiveness and accuracy of formative assessment in Key Stage 1.

- What do you think the key challenges might be in the process of transforming assessment in Key Stage 1?
- What changes might need to be implemented to pedagogi-cal approaches to accommodate observational assessment in Key Stage 1?

 Reflective Activity

You work in a Year 2 classroom and, to date, past test papers (Statutory Assessment Tests) have been the key instrument to assess children's attainment. Alongside your colleagues, you have implemented systems that focus heavily on formative observa-tional assessment. These systems build on the assessment processes used in effective EYFS settings. As a Year 2 practitioner, you know how well these approaches support robust professional judgements in relation to individual attainment in the core sub-jects. They also aid you in identifying clear next steps in learning. Several parents have approached you and questioned your approach to assessment. They are clearly unfamiliar with these informal methods of collecting evidence. The parents appear to be more interested in levels of attainment than in having knowl-edge of what their children have achieved and how they can be supported to move forward in their learning. How would you address this issue with the parents, whilst retaining the systems you have implemented?

Case Study: Involving parents in assessment beyond the Foundation Stage

Read the following case study and think about the types of assessment evidence which parents or carers might collect from the learning that takes place at home.

In School Y, parents' and carers' contributions to the assessment process in the EYFS had been effectively embedded. Through discussion, parents were familiar with their child's attainment and future learning needs. The setting had acknowledged that learning takes place at both home and school. Parents had been encouraged to celebrate their child's achievements at home by completing a certificate, with details of individual achievement. These certificates were then displayed in the setting and later transferred as evidence of attainment to the child's learning journey.

As this cohort transferred to Year 1, it was the parents who initially transferred this system. They asked the practitioner for certificates to acknowledge achievement within the home and clearly expected that systems embedded in EYFS practice would continue into Key Stage 1. The school acknowledged that this was a very reasonable expectation on the part of the parents. Since the national focus is to report achievement in the core subjects at the end of Key Stage 1, it was decided that, initially, parents would contribute to the assessment process in these areas.

Parents were invited to an information meeting and advised that their contributions relating to their child's achievements at home would continue to be welcomed and celebrated in Key Stage 1 settings. The practitioners in Key Stage 1 had developed learning journeys for each child to track achievements in the core subjects, as well as achievements in personal, social, health and citizenship education. Attainment in speaking and listening was also evidenced. Achievements relating to any of these curriculum areas were discussed with parents and children. The practitioners then referenced this evidence to National Curriculum levels and included this information in individual learning journeys. School Y considered the broad-level descriptions unhelpful for identifying children's next steps in learning. The school referred to available documentation, relating to National Curriculum levels, to identify small, achievable next steps in learning in the core subjects. Currently, documentation to support children's next steps has been replaced with the APP materials from the National Strategies. Parents regularly contribute to the assessment process and, through discussion with practitioners, are able to identify next steps in learning.

- What types of assessment evidence might parents or carers collect from their child's learning at home?
- How might you support your colleagues in Key Stage 1 to help them recognise the importance of parental contributions to the assessment process?

Effective transition

Sanders et al. (2005) carried out research on the transition between the Foundation Stage and Key Stage 1. They found that Year 1 teachers experienced difficulties in developing play-based approaches to learning due to the expectations placed on them to deliver more structured learning through the literacy and mathematics strategies. The researchers found that transition was more problematic for younger children, children with SEN, and children with EAL. For these children, transition caused anxiety. The research recommended that Year 1 practitioners should consider adopting similar routines and pedagogical approaches to those used in the Foundation Stage. In particular, Year 1 teachers were advised to increase opportunities for active, independent learning and continue to provide the play experiences offered in the Foundation Stage.

This research is important because it stresses the necessity for Year 1 teachers to adopt similar pedagogical approaches to those used in the Foundation Stage. This has implications for the way in which learning is assessed in Year 1. Rich, play-based contexts for learning in Year 1 open up new possibilities for observational assessment and opportunities for collecting evidence in a range of forms.

- What do you think are the benefits of a smooth transition?

- What are the key challenges for practitioners in Year 1?

- How might these challenges be overcome?

- How can colleagues in the Foundation Stage support their colleagues in Year 1?

Seamless approaches to teaching, learning and assessment between the Foundation Stage and Year 1 enable the child's learning journey to continue. Assessment via formal testing in Year 1 is wholly inappropriate and lacks validity. It is decontextualised and stressful for children. Formal testing only catches a glimpse of what children know and can do. It cannot capture the full extent of a child's learning. Effective teachers in any age should be able to pinpoint what stage children are at in their learning without the need for formal assessments. Effective practitioners have an in-depth knowledge about their learners. This knowledge base is formulated on the basis of daily observations of children's independent learning, discussions with the child's parent or carer, conversations with the child, scrutiny of samples of recorded work, and photographic evidence. Effective practitioners document the learning within context. If practitioners adopt these approaches to assessment, there will be no purpose or need for any form of formal assessment.

Further Reading

Qualifications and Curriculum Authority (2008) *Continuing the Learning Journey: Training Package.* QCA.

- This is an updated version of the original version of this document and contains excellent training for Year 1 teachers. The package includes examples of best practice for transition from EYFS to Key Stage 1.

Useful Websites

http://nationalstrategies.standards.dcsf.gov.uk/primary/assessment/assessing pupilsprogressapp

- This site provides detailed guidance on the use of the APP materials to track children's attainment in Key Stages 1 and 2. The APP materials focus on the importance of continuous teacher assessment and reflect elements of best practice in the EYFS.

References

Athey, C. (2007) *Extending Thought in Young Children: A Parent–Teacher Partnership*. London: Paul Chapman.

Bayley, R. et al. (2008) *Like Bees, Not Butterflies*. London: A & C Black.

Billington, T. (2000) *Separating, Losing and Excluding Children: Narratives of Difference*. London: Routledge Falmer.

Bilton, H. (1998) *Outdoor Play in the Early Years*. London: David Fulton.

Booth, T., Ainscow, M., Black-Hawkins, K., Vaughan, M. and Shaw, L. (2000) *Index for Inclusion*. Bristol: Centre for Studies on Inclusive Education.

Bronfenbrenner, U. (1979) *The Ecology of Human Development: Experiments by Nature and Design*. London: Harvard University Press.

Brooker, L. (2008) *Supporting Transition in the Early Years*. Maidenhead: Open University Press.

Browne, N. (2004) *Gender Equity in the Early Years*. Maidenhead: Open University Press/McGraw-Hill Education.

Bruce, T. (1987) *Early Childhood Education*. London: Hodder & Stoughton.

Bruce, T. (2001) *Learning Through Play*. Dubai: Hodder Education.

Carr, M. (2001) *Assessment in Early Childhood Settings: Learning Stories*. London: Paul Chapman.

Carr, M. (2007) *Assessment in Early Childhood Settings: Learning Stories*. London: Sage.

Clark, A. and Moss, P. (2001) *Listening to Young Children: The Mosaic Approach*. National Children's Bureau and Joseph Rowntree Foundation.

Corbett, J. (2001) 'Teaching Approaches Which Support Inclusive Education: A Connective Pedagogy', *British Journal of Special Education*, 28 (2): 55–59.

Corbett, J. and Slee, R. (2000) 'An International Conversation on Inclusive Education', in F. Armstrong, D. Armstrong and L. Barton (eds), *Inclusive Education: Policy Contexts and Comparative Perspectives*. London: David Fulton.

Dahlberg, G. and Moss, P. (2005) *Ethics and Politics in Early Childhood Education*. London: Routledge Falmer.

Dahlberg, G., Moss, P. and Pence, A. (1999) *Beyond Quality in Early Childhood Education and Care: Postmodern Perspectives*. London: Falmer Press.

Daly, M. et al. (2006) *Understanding Early Years Theory in Practice*. Oxford: Heinemann.

Department for Children, Schools and Families (DCSF) (2007) *The Children's Plan: Building Brighter Futures*. London: HMSO.

Department for Children, Schools and Families (DCSF) (2007a) *Confident, Capable and Creative: Supporting Boys' Achievements: Guidance for Practitioners in the Early Years Foundation Stage*. Nottingham: DCSF.

Department for Children, Schools and Families (DCSF) (2008) *The Early Years Foundation Stage: Setting the Standards for Learning Development and Care for Children from Birth to Five*. Nottingham: DCSF.

Department for Children, Schools and Families (DCSF) (2008a) *The Early Years Foundation Stage: The Statutory Framework*. Nottingham: DCSF.

Department for Children, Schools and Families (DCSF) (2008b) *The Early Years Foundation Stage: The practice guidance*. Nottingham: DCSF.

Department for Children, Schools and Families (DCSF) (2008c) *The Early Years Foundation Stage: Principles into Practice Cards*. Nottingham: DCSF.

Department for Education and Science (DES) (1978) *Report of the Committee of Enquiry into the Education of Handicapped Children and Young People*. London: HMSO.

Department for Education and Skills (DfES) (2000) *Curriculum Guidance for the Foundation Stage*. Nottingham: DfES.

Department for Education and Skills (DfES) (2001) *Special Educational Needs Code of Practice*. Nottingham: DfES.

Department for Education and Skills (DfES) (2002) *Birth to Three Matters – a Framework to Support Children in Their Earliest Years*. Nottingham: DfES.

Department for Education and Skills (DfES) (2003) *National Standards for Under Eights Day Care and Childminding*. Nottingham: DfES.

Department for Education and Skills (DfES) (2004) *Every Child Matters: Change for Children*. Nottingham: DfES.

Department for Education and Skills (DfES) (2004a) *Removing Barriers to Achievement: The Government Strategy for SEN*. Nottingham: DfES.

Department for Education and Skills (DfES) (2005) *Common Core of Skills and Knowledge for the Children's Workforce*. Nottingham: DfES.

Devereux, J. and Miller, L. (2003) *Working with Children in the Early Years*. London: David Fulton.

Donaldson, M. (1978) *Children's Minds*. London: Fontana.

Drake, J. (2005) *Planning Children's Learning in the Foundation Stage*, 2nd edn. London: David Fulton.

Drummond, M. J. (1993) *Assessing Children's Learning*. London: David Fulton.

Drummond, M. J. (2003) *Assessing Children's Learning*, 2nd edn. London: David Fulton.

Dunkin, D. and Hanna, P. (2001) *Thinking Together; Quality Adult: Child interactions*. Wellington, New Zealand: NZCER Distribution Services.

Edgington, M. (2004) *The Foundation Stage Teacher in Action*, 3rd edn. London: Paul Chapman.

Elfer, P., Goldschmied, E. and Selleck, D. (2003) *Key Persons in the Nursery: Building Relationships for Quality Provision*. London: David Fulton.

Farquhar, S. E. (2003) Child Forum Research Network: Quality Teaching: Early Foundations Best Evidence Synthesis. Wellington, New Zealand, Ministry of Education.

Fisher, J. (2004) *Starting from the Child*, 2nd edn. Buckingham: Open University Press.

Florian, L. (1998) 'An Examination of the Practical Problems Associated with the Implementation of Inclusive Education Policies', *Support for Learning*, 13 (3): 105–108.

Foucault, M. (1972) *The Archaeology of Knowledge*. London: Tavistock Publications.

Foucault, M. (1980) *Power/Knowledge*. Brighton: Harvester.

Gettinger, M. and Stoiber, K. C. (1998) 'Critical Incident Recording: A Procedure for Monitoring Children's Performance and Maximising Progress in Inclusive Settings', *Early Childhood Education Journal*, 26 (1): 39–46 in Carr, M. (2001) *Assessment in Early Childhood Settings: Learning Stories*. London: SAGE.

Gmitrova, V. and Gmitrov, J. (2003) 'The Impact of Teacher-Directed and Child-Directed Pretend Play on Cognitive Competence in Kindergarten Children', *Early Childhood Education*, 30 (4): 241–246.

Goldschmied, E. and Jackson, S. (2004) *People Under Three: Young Children in Day Care*, 2nd edn. London: Routledge.

Goldstein, L. S. (2008) 'Teaching the Standards Is Developmentally Appropriate Practice: Strategies for Incorporating the Sociopolitical Dimension of DAP in Early Childhood Teaching', *Early Childhood Education*, 36 (3): 253–260.

Gura, P. and Hall, L. (2000) 'Self Assesssment', *Early Years Educator*, June 2000.

Hamilton, C. et al. (2003) *Principles and Practice in the Foundation Stage*. Exeter: Learning Matters.

HM Government (2004) *Every Child Matters: Change for Children*. HM Government.

Hughes, A. M. (2006) *Developing Play for the Under Threes: The Treasure Basket and Heuristic Play*. London: David Fulton.

Hutchin, V. (1999) *Right From the Start. Effective Planning and Assessment in the Early Years*. London: Hodder and Stoughton.

Hutchin, V. (2000) *Tracking Significant Achievement in the Early Years*, 2nd edn. London: Hodder and Stoughton.

Hutchin, V. (2003) *Observing and Assessing for the Foundation Stage Profile*. London: Hodder and Stoughton.

Hutchin, V. (2007) *Supporting Every Child's Learning Across the Early Years Foundation Stage*. London: Hodder Education.

Keating, I. (2007) *Teaching Foundation Stage*. Exeter: Learning Matters.

Kelly, B. (1992) 'Concepts of Assessment: An Overview of Progression, Observation and Assessment in Early Education' in G. M. Blenkin and A. Kelly (eds), *Assessment in Early Childhood Education*. London: Paul Chapman (pp. 1–25).

Laevers, F. (ed.) (1996) *An Exploration of the Concept of Involvement as an Indicator for Quality in Early Childhood Education*. Dundee: Scottish Consultative Council on the Curriculum.

Lancaster, P. and Broadbent, V. (2005) *Listening to Young Children* (the pack). Maidenhead: McGraw-Hill Education.

Lave, J. and Wenger, E. (1998) *Communities of Practice: Learning, Meaning and Identity*. Cambridge: Cambridge University Press.

Lindon, J. (2006) *Helping Babies and Toddlers Learn: A Guide to Good Practice with Under-Threes*. London: National Children's Bureau.

MacNaughton, G. (2003) *Shaping Early Childhood: Learners, Curriculum and Contexts*. Maidenhead: Open University Press.

MacNaughton, G. (2005) *Doing Foucault in Early Childhood Studies: Applying Poststructural Ideas*. Abingdon: Routledge.

MacNaughton, G. and Williams, G. (2008) *Teaching Young Children: Choices in Theory and Practice*. Maidenhead: Open University Press.

MacNaughton, G. and Williams, G. (2009) *Teaching Young Children: Choices in Theory and Practice*, 2nd edn. Maidenhead: Open University Press.

Malaguzzi, L. (1993) 'No Way – the Hundred Is There', cited in C. Edwards, L. Gandini and G. Forman (eds), *The Hundred Languages of Children: The Reggio Emilia Approach to Early Childhood Education*. Norwood, NJ: Ablex.

Malaguzzi, L. (1996) *The Hundred Languages of Children: A Narrative of the Possible (catalogue of the exhibit), Reggio Emilia, Italy: Reggio Children*, cited in J. Devereux and L. Miller (2003), *Working with Children in the Early Years*. London: David Fulton.

Marsh, J. (ed.) (2005) *Popular Culture, New Media and Digital Literacy in Early Childhood*. Abingdon: Routlege Falmer.

Miller, L., Cable, C. and Devereux, J. (2005) *Developing Early Years Practice*. London: David Fulton.

Morrison, G. (2009) *Early Childhood Education Today*, 11th edn. Upper Saddle River, NJ: Pearson Education.

National Assessment Agency (2008) *Engaging Parents and Children in EYFS*. Profile Assessment, NAA.

Nutbrown, C. (2006) *Threads of Thinking: Young Children Learning and the Role of Early Education*, 3rd edn. London: Paul Chapman.

Ofsted (2008) *The Foundation Stage: A Report of 144 Settings*. HMI 2610, available on www.ofsted.gov.uk.

Palaiologou, I. (2008) *Childhood Observation*. Exeter: Learning Matters.

Palmer, S. (2007) *Toxic Childhood*. London: Orion.

Pascal, C. and Bertram, T. (1997) *Effective Early Learning: Case Studies in Improvement*. London: Paul Chapman.

Porter, L. (2003) *Young Children's Behaviour: Practical Approaches for Carergivers and Teachers*, 2nd edn. London: Paul Chapman.

Post, J. and Hohmann, M. (2000) *Tender Care and Early Learning: Supporting Infants and Toddlers in Child Care Settings*. Ypsilanti, MI: High Scope.

Qualifications and Curriculum Authority (QCA) (2008) *The Early Years Foundation Stage Profile Handbook*. London: QCA.

Rawlings, A. (2008) *Studying Early Years: A Guide to Work-Based Learning*. Maidenhead: McGraw-Hill/Open University Press.

Rinaldi, C. (1995) 'The Emergent Curriculum and Social Constructivism: An Interview with Lella Gandini', in C. Edwards, L. Gandini and G. Forman (eds), *The Hundred Languages of Children: The Reggio Emilia Approach to Early Childhood Education*. Norwood, NJ: Ablex.

Rinaldi, C. (2006) *In Dialogue with Reggio Emilia: Listening, Researching and Learning*. Abingdon: Routledge.

Roberts, R. (2002) *Self Esteem and Early Learning*, 3rd edn. London: Paul Chapman.

Robinson, M. (2008) *Child Development from Birth to Eight: A Journey Through the Early Years*. Maidenhead: Open University Press.

Rogoff, B. (1999) 'Cognitive Development Through Social Interaction', in P. Murphy (ed.), *Learning and Assessment*. London: Paul Chapman.

Sanders, D., White, G., Burge, B., Sharp, C., Eames, A., McCure, R. and Grayson, H. (2005) *A Study of the Transition from the Foundation Stage to Key Stage 1*. Sure Start. Nottingham: DfES.

Schon, D. (1987) *Educating the Reflective Practitioner: Towards a New Design for Teaching in the Professions*. Oxford: Jossey-Bass.

Sylva, K., Melhuish, E., Sammons, P., Siraj-Blatchford, I. and Taggart, B. (2004) *The Effective Provision of Pre-School Education (EPPE)*. London: DfES.

Siraj-Blatchford, I. and Clarke, P. (2000) *Supporting Identity, Diversity and Language in Early Years*. Buckingham: Open University Press.

Siraj-Blatchford, I., Sylva, K., Muttock, S., Gildon, R. and Bell, D. (2002) *Researching Effective Pedagogy in the Early Years: Research Report 356*. Norwich: DfES/HMSO.

Slee, P. and Shute, R. (2003) *Child Development: Thinking About Theories*. London: Arnold.

Stroh, K. and Robinson, T. (1998) 'Learning and Communication: Functional Learning Programmes for Young Developmentally Delayed Children', in A. M. Hughes (ed.), (2006) *Developing Play for the Under Threes: The Treasure Basket and Heuristic Play*. London: David Fulton.

Thomas, G., Walker, D. and Webb, J., (1998) *The Making of the Inclusive School*. London: Routledge.

Torrance, H. and Pryor, J. (1998) *Investing Formative Assessment: Teaching Learning and Assessment in the Classroom*. Buckingham: Open University Press.

Trawick-Smith, J. (1998) 'A Qualitative Analysis of Metaplay in the Pre-school Years' *Early Childhood Education Research Quarterly* Vol. 9, No. 1, pp. 433–452.

Tregaskis, C. (2002) 'Social Model Theory: the story so far...', *Disability and Society,* 17 (4): 457–470.

UNESCO (1994) The Salamanca Statement and Framework for Action on Special Needs Education: World Conference on Special Needs: Access and Quality, US Department of Education.

United Nations (1989) The Convention on the Rights of the Child: Adopted by the General Assembly of the United Nations, 20 November.

Vygotsky, L. (1978) *Mind in Society*. Cambridge, MA: Harvard University Press.

Whalley, M. (2008) *Leading Practice in Early Years Settings*. Exeter: Learning Matters.

Wood, E. and Attfield, J. (2005) *Play, Learning and the Early Childhood Curriculum*. London: Paul Chapman.

Index

Added to a page number 'f' denotes a figure and 't' denotes a table.

Assessment for Learning
in the Early Years
Foundation Stage

Education at SAGE

SAGE is a leading international publisher of journals, books, and electronic media for academic, educational, and professional markets.

Our education publishing includes:

- accessible and comprehensive texts for aspiring education professionals and practitioners looking to further their careers through continuing professional development

- inspirational advice and guidance for the classroom

- authoritative state of the art reference from the leading authors in the field

Find out more at: **www.sagepub.co.uk/education**